UPGRADE YOUR LEADERSHIP

ERIC PFEIFFER

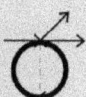

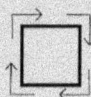

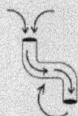

ISBN: 978-1-7373414-5-1(PB)
ISBN: 978-1-7373414-6-8 (eBook)

Printed in the United States of America

Published by Gravitas House

GH
GRAVITAS HOUSE

www.gravitashouse.com

Edited by Suzanne Lathrop
Interior design and art by Olivier Darbonville
Cover design by Think Deeper, LLC (thinkdeeper.com)

UPGRADE YOUR LEADERSHIP

8 Foundational Tools to
Overcome Drama, Build Trust,
and Thrive Under Pressure

ERIC PFEIFFER

CONTENTS

THE JOURNEY AHEAD

Welcome to *The MPWR Leadership Toolkit*, or what we refer to as our Leadership Operating System. At MPWR Coaching, we have spent years developing a leadership system that empowers individuals, teams and entire organizations for sustainable success. In other words, what you will find in this book is an opportunity to upgrade your Leadership Operating System. This book is a guide designed to help you unlock your full leadership potential and empower those around you to do the same. Whether you're a seasoned executive, an emerging leader, or someone simply looking to level up in life, this book is for you.

True leadership is not about rank or status. It's about influence, impact, and creating environments where people can thrive.

Leadership is often misunderstood as a position or title. But true leadership is not about rank or status. It's about influence, impact, and creating environments where people can thrive. It's about overcoming drama, building trust, developing others, and empowering your team to achieve more than any person can do on their own.

When I first started my leadership journey, I made the same mistake many of us do—I thought leadership was about being in control, calling the shots, and making sure people followed my vision. But the truth is, leadership is far less about you and far more about the people you lead. The best leaders aren't dictators—they're facilitators, enablers, and coaches. The best leaders understand their primary job is to be a leader worth following, elevating those around them. After all, we're only as good as our teams.

That's why I created the *MPWR Leadership Toolkit*—to provide leaders like you with practical, actionable tools that will help you become the kind of leader who doesn't just get the job done, but transforms the people and the culture around them in the process. We can accomplish far greater things when we work well together.

What This Book Is About

This book is built on a simple, but powerful, idea: Leadership is a system. Much like a device's operating system quietly powers a computer, smartphone or tablet, whatever leadership system you have in place empowers (or doesn't) your ability to achieve increased productivity and profitability. And I'm not just talking about financial profitability. If someone asked your team whether they profit from being part of your business, would they brag about more than a sufficient paycheck? The tools revealed in this book provide the most powerful leadership system, ensuring that you have everything you need to:

- Be a leader worth following
- Cultivate high-performing teams
- Overcome toxicity and dysfunction
- Operate sustainably
- Drive meaningful results.

In Section 1, we'll explore how our computing devices are an incredible metaphor to help us understand the need to continually upgrade how we lead in any context. We'll begin by recognizing the power source of any team or company—its people and how they operate. We'll also look at the importance of understanding that *how* people do what they do is as important, if not more important, than *what* they do. We'll finish the first chapters by establishing the cornerstone of any good leadership system, the power of personal responsibility.

Section 2 will introduce the *MPWR Leadership Toolkit* (also known as our Leadership Operating System). At MPWR Coaching, we understand it's not enough to tell leaders what to do; we must provide a simple, repeatable framework to ensure predictable growth and greater achievements. Each chapter in this section introduces a new leadership tool, focusing on essential principles and practices for developing an empowered culture. From emotional intelligence to productivity, trust to development, these tools will help you diagnose, upgrade, and fine-tune the leadership systems that are already in place in your life and work. Each tool is designed to give you clarity, provide direction, and lead to practical breakthroughs—whether for yourself, your team, or your organization.

Why You Need This Book

If you've ever felt like leadership is more difficult than it should be—like you're raking water uphill or constantly putting out fires—you're not alone. The truth is most of us weren't taught how to lead. We're handed the title, given the keys to the office, and expected to figure it out as we go.

Perhaps you've digested countless books, podcasts, or webinars on leadership and still feel ill-equipped for the challenges before you. Again, you're not alone. Leadership shouldn't be a mystery or magic show. It can be learned and excelled in by anyone. We can all become capable and effective leaders. With the right tools and practice, you can become a leader worth following and also enjoy the journey along the way. This book will teach you how to:

- Bring the best version of yourself
- Build a culture of trust and collaboration
- Get the best from your team members
- Thrive in unpredictable environments
- Stay productive, all while staying true to your authentic self.

Consider this: we wouldn't think of climbing Mt. Everest without the right tools, equipment and a guide to help us ensure a successful journey. This book represents the tools you'll need to scale

Leadership shouldn't be a mystery or magic show.

new heights. They have empowered thousands before you, so you can trust them. Many of the chapters will offer practical exercises and handles so you can implement the ideas into your everyday life and experience real traction and forward movement. And if you're looking for a guide, someone to help you get to the top of your summit, don't hesitate to reach out to us at MPWR Coaching. We won't carry you to the top, but we'll certainly give you the best chance of getting there!

Throughout my career, I've seen firsthand how transformative it can be to have a guide—someone who's been down the road before and can help you navigate leadership challenges and opportunities. The best leaders are not necessarily the smartest or most skilled, but those who ask for help and commit themselves to their craft. If you find yourself resonating with the content in this book and you're ready to take your leadership to the next level, I invite you to connect with our team. At MPWR Coaching, we specialize in helping leaders like you unlock their potential and create environments that thrive amidst the chaos. Coaching isn't about telling you what to do—it's about equipping you with practical tools and strategies that best empower you and your team to unlock a better future.

Leadership is a journey, not a destination. And like any journey worth taking, it's better with a trusted guide by your side.

How to Use This Book

As you go through each chapter of this book, you'll encounter actionable insights, real-world examples, and tools you can implement immediately. By the end of the book, you'll have a comprehensive leadership toolkit that fuels clarity and confidence to tackle the mountains ahead of you with courage. You'll know the secret to upgrading your leadership system so that you have the competitive advantage you've been looking for. You'll have the skills to build a culture of trust, develop high-performing teams, and cultivate a leadership style that is authentic, powerful, and sustainable.

The contents of this book are the core foundation we use in our MPWR Coaching process. Therefore, take your time. This book isn't meant to be consumed willy-nilly. Take notes, wrestle with the ideas, and ask the hard question: *If I implement these actionable insights, will it upgrade my leadership abilities?* Test everything and stick with what resonates. Move forward with what you believe will help you take your leadership to new heights!

Let's get started.

PART ONE

~~~~~~~~~~~~~~~~~~~~

THE ENGINE OF BUSINESS

01

THE ENGINE OF EVERY BUSINESS: PEOPLE

B ob was something of a mathematical genius and had overseen the finances of a promising young company from its inception. He was part of the founding team that built a humble food commodities distribution service into a billion-dollar national juggernaut. In those early days, fewer than twenty people were responsible for distributing pallets of refined flour, totes of baking mixes, and drums of cooking oils to large-scale bakeries across the southwest of the US. Fast-forward forty years, and the company has become one of the nation's leading distributors of raw commodities to the largest and most well-known food production outlets.

Bob had been instrumental in the company's financial journey. But now, on an unusually rainy day in Los Angeles, he found himself sitting across the table from myself and the company's president. The president had brought me in to assess the senior leadership team and determine what it would take to cross a new threshold of success. The uncomfortable reality? Bob had proven himself to be a liability.

Bob was brilliant with numbers and had guided the company through numerous financial hardships. However, there was a glaring problem: no one enjoyed working with Bob. He was brash, belittling, and condescending—not only to his team, but also to his superiors. He hoarded information as a power play and was quick to dismiss or undermine others who challenged his perspective. Bob's talent with numbers couldn't compensate for his inability to collaborate, and as the company grew, his toxic behavior became a bigger issue.

As we sat across the table from one another, I asked, "Bob, help me understand something. You're clearly very capable when it comes to running the numbers, but why are there so many complaints about how you interact with your team, colleagues, and even your superiors?" Bob stared at me for a moment before replying, "I think they're intimidated by my intelligence."

"Ok," I said. "But if you're going to lead the finance team for this company, don't you think it might be helpful to ensure your direct reports feel like they're part of your team? And don't you think the owners want to feel confident entrusting you with the financial future of this company?" Bob's face grew visibly angry. He suddenly retorted, "All I do is make sure this company doesn't go belly up. I'm tired of carrying it on my back. Without me, this company would be in a ditch!"

I had seen this before, so I knew where to take the conversation. I replied, "Bob, despite your many abilities, it seems very few people enjoy working with you." He quickly shot back, "That's not my fault. I can't help it if they don't know how to run a company!" And there it was: With all that Bob brought to this company, he hadn't realized he had become more of a liability than an asset.

We've all worked with someone like Bob. They're talented, but they think everyone else is the problem. They can't take personal responsibility, they deflect blame and are convinced if everyone else were just like them, everything would be better. We all have blind spots, but when those blind spots lead to self-protecting behaviors, we find ourselves unable to acknowledge where we need to change. Few things make me sadder than when someone has become their own worst enemy.

The irony is that the leadership of this organization desperately wanted to see things work with Bob. They wanted to see him grow with the business, but at some point, no matter how talented someone is, an individual is never more important than the team or organization.

Empowered People Power Business

Here's one of the most overlooked factors in the success of any business: The engine of every business is its people. When people are operating well, individually and collectively, our business thrives. And when they don't, the business doesn't. Simple as that. So, when was the last time you slowed down to ask, "How is our engine running?"

I've spent years and countless hours helping organizations effectively diagnose and upgrade the way their people operate.

The engine of your business— how your people operate, individually and collectively— deeply matters to your bottom line.

Sadly, most wait until they're exasperated, stuck and deeply frustrated, before asking for help. Others have become discouraged after hiring multiple consultants and coaches, only to find they haven't moved the needle. Nevertheless, the strength of how your people operate will determine your business's ability to grow, scale, function well, and thrive amid challenges. The engine of your business—how your people operate, individually and collectively—deeply matters to your bottom line.

Like Bob, every person has developed their own way of operating. Remember, Bob brought some incredibly helpful qualities to this team. That's not the problem. The problem is that Bob also operated in ways that were toxic and destructive to relationships. His strengths did not outweigh his weaknesses. And this is the conundrum I run into often— we hire for skill and fire for character.

Let me explain.

In workplace culture, we have tended to celebrate skill over character. As I said before, we hire for skill and then lament that same person's lack of ability to work effectively with others. By character I'm referring to *how* people do *what* they do. Bob was very talented at running numbers and creating immaculate spreadsheets, but his presence in the workplace was alienating everyone around him.

The way people work to solve problems, make decisions, and partner in achieving their goals is always an expression of their core values, expectations, self-perception, and how they see their role within any context. This is character: HOW we do WHAT we do. Sadly, I'm rarely brought into companies because they're lacking competent individuals. More often, I'm brought in because there are competent individuals who undercut the culture by how they operate. This is often the byproduct of multiple people operating from different expectations and standards.

Every person within a business brings their own personal set of behavioral standards, their own "playbook"—their idea of how things should work. Now, imagine trying to get a team to communicate effectively, solve problems, and move forward together when they're all functioning from different playbooks. Chaos, right? That is no different than trying to run multiple operating systems on a single computing device. It doesn't work.

This is the predicament for most of the leaders, teams, and companies I work with. They're deeply frustrated by the failures of people working together and even more frustrated by their own deficiencies to diagnose and fix the problem. Toxic attitudes, dysfunctions, and unresolved conflicts run rampant, while leaders feel exhausted, perplexed, and without solutions. Whether we're dealing with difficult individuals or a team that can't synchronize, the problem is the same—we need an upgraded leadership system.

You're Not Alone

Perhaps you resonate with Bob's story. Perhaps you resonate with the leader who has a Bob or two on their team. Either way, you're not alone. I can assure you that I've never worked with a leader or team who didn't have a bit of *Bob* in them. No matter our age or experience, we all have areas of how we engage our environment that need to change. The sooner we realize we all have deficiencies in how we operate, the sooner we can choose to embark on a journey of transformation.

The vast majority of leaders I've worked with eventually concede to feeling "impostor syndrome." It's that sneaking suspicion that we'll be found out, that we don't really know what we're doing, and that our life, team or business will falter because of our lack of leadership ability. Do you fear someone will find out you're not quite sure what to do? Does it ever keep you up at night, wondering if you'll figure it out?

Before you start beating yourself up, let me offer some perspective. First, the vast majority of leaders in any position were not intentionally trained for their leadership responsibilities (that includes parenting!). Add to that, the traditional education system doesn't teach much by way of leadership skills, as if the only way to learn it is through trial by fire. All this to say, you're in good company. Every leader should feel at least a bit of impostor syndrome; it helps keep our egos in check and makes way for continuous growth and development, vital traits in the ever-changing leadership landscape.

Bob was talented in various skills, but leadership was not one of them. And his unwillingness to recognize this deficiency or engage in any leadership training was costing him much more than a job. Sure, he showed up for many of the leadership training sessions, but entrenched himself with an arrogant and condescending posture. Bob was sacrificing a better future for himself and others on the altar of his need to be right and protect his fragile ego. In leadership, our options are to grow or stagnate. We can either put in the work to become a greater asset or devolve into a liability. My team spent months trying to help Bob upgrade his ability to lead himself and others, but there are two questions everyone must wrestle with when aspiring to become a better leader: (1) *Am I willing to recognize my need for growth?* and (2) *Am I willing to do the work?*

The point of this story isn't to throw Bob under the bus, but to give us a chance to identify the Bob in each of us. None of us are perfect and none of us have "arrived." We're all works in progress. Each of us can become better leaders by upgrading how we operate. Will we recognize our deficiencies? Will we give ourselves permission to become a better version of ourselves? Will we aspire to greater influence and impact? Will we do the work to become a leader worth following and learn to build a culture where everyone can thrive?

I approach this conversation with incredible empathy and compassion because I have oftentimes had to confront the "Bob" in me.

Anything Worth Doing is Worth Doing Poorly

I first realized I wanted to be a leader in my mid-twenties. While celebrating with a small team I was part of that had successfully launched a new initiative within our organization, I remember hearing the CEO lavish our team leader with high praise. It was then I knew I wanted to be a leader. Shortly after, I was promoted to lead a small team of my own. The thought of trying my hand at leadership was exhilarating, yet it only took a few short weeks before I realized how far in over my head I was.

My boss called me into her office to let me know the team wasn't responding well to my leadership. I felt shocked and immediately shot back, "I'm doing everything I can to lead well. Maybe they're just having a hard time keeping up." She looked at me intently, her eyes wincing, as if she had dealt with this kind of situation many times. "Eric," she kindly started, "I know you're new to leadership, so I'll say this gently. You're only a leader if others are following you. You have a great team. They're not the problem. You are." Like so many other areas of my life, to become more of an asset, I first had to own where I was a liability!

Listen carefully: We cannot blame others for our leadership inadequacies. Even the highest-level leaders I work with find themselves tempted to deflect blame onto others when things are

After all, we can only give to others **what we first cultivate within ourselves.**

not going well. Strong leaders, however, always look at themselves first. The change we want to see in our teams and organizations always begins with the work we do on ourselves. It is our responsibility as leaders to invest the time, energy, and resources into elevating our own leadership capacity. After all, we can only give to others what we first cultivate within ourselves.

I despised what my boss was sharing with me. I wanted to be a great leader but recoiled at the fact that I wasn't one yet. This was the beginning of learning that to become great at anything, you have to suck first. I know—not the encouraging leadership talk we're all hoping for, but it's true. To grow, mature and become an expert in any discipline, we have to stumble, fumble and bumble our way into it. During this time, I took solace from this quote, "Anything worth doing is worth doing poorly [until we get better]."[1]

Unless we want to end up in Bob's predicament, we need a simple, repeatable and sustainable way to continually upgrade our leadership abilities!

Upgrade your Leadership

If high-capacity leadership is genuinely attainable, why do some leaders plateau while others seem to be on a constant upward trajectory? In other words, how do we maintain our journey of becoming increasingly greater assets to any leadership responsibility? In the same way that we're constantly upgrading our

---

1   G.K. Chesterton, *What's Wrong with the World,* 1910

> In the same way that we're constantly upgrading our smartphones to ensure optimal performance, **we need a way to continually upgrade our leadership performance.**

smartphones to ensure optimal performance, we need a way to continually upgrade our leadership performance.

Let me explain.

We love our digital devices because we can open up an app to help us navigate our finances, weight loss journey, or directions to a new restaurant. While one app tracks our sleep patterns, another gives us access to our favorite streaming shows. Each app represents a solution to a specific problem or desire, but these apps are only useful because of the operating system empowering them.

A smartphone's operating system is the parental software that ensures the hard ware, software and user experience are integrated and optimized. Can you imagine using the same operating system today that came with our first smartphones? There have been countless upgrades to these operating systems to keep up with new applications and the demands of the user. Now, let's lay this metaphor over our leadership experience.

Every leadership book, podcast, or article we digest is like downloading a new leadership app. We download all these leadership apps and still feel woefully under-equipped to handle the typical drama that inevitably pops up in our workplace dynamics. Can you relate to any of the following:

1. John continues to withhold pertinent information from the sales team.

2. Kim still bashes her counterpart from another division over an unspoken feud that started six months ago.

3. Steve can't get his team to trust him due to his passive-aggressive behaviors.

4. Juliette is convinced her pleas for part-time remote work will never be truly considered and is already looking for an escape route.

Our frustration isn't primarily due to a lack of good leadership ideas, but to our lack of understanding how to integrate and apply these ideas effectively. We need a practical and accessible way to upgrade our Leadership Operating System—how we influence and impact our environment. We need a simple, internal framework that enhances and empowers how we respond to life experiences, so that we're operating from greater composure and serving the best interests of those involved. And who doesn't want that?

We need a simple, internal framework that enhances and empowers how we respond to life experiences, so that we're operating from greater composure and serving the best interests of those involved. And who doesn't want that?

We All Have a Personal Operating System, But is it Working?

Every person has developed their own personal operating system from their earliest years. Like a smartphone, our operating system is comprised of the guiding paradigms, beliefs, attitudes, and behaviors that govern the way we understand and respond to our experiences. We inherit part of our operating system from our upbringing. Other parts were developed through our time in school, sports teams, various jobs, books we've read, mentors, and the like. Through all these experiences, we adopted various mindsets and behavioral patterns we believed would help us navigate the challenges we faced. Parts of our operating system have proven helpful, yielding productive responses, while others have proven unhelpful, yielding harmful and unwanted outcomes.

My father's anger issues were part of the operating system he inherited from his childhood. If the kids were being loud, he believed yelling at us would fix the problem. From him I learned that anger and physical intimidation were a way of controlling my environment. If my mom didn't want to talk to someone who called, she asked us to tell a trivial lie on her behalf. From her I learned to avoid uncomfortable conversations. In order to protect my ego in sports, I often pretended like I wasn't giving my all so I always had an excuse for underperforming. These attitudes and behaviors are each reflective of our personal operating system. In other words, our operating system is represented by the prevailing attitudes and behaviors through which we engage our lives. And I can assure you, our behaviors don't lie. They always reveal our operating system...for better or worse.

Once we realize that every person on our team or in our business is running their own operating system, it isn't difficult to imagine the challenges that will inevitably ensue. Each person has their own way of seeing, interpreting, and responding to any number of situations. One person handles conflict with aggressive language and shouting, while another avoids conflict like the plague. One person always feels the need to have an answer, while another regularly shies away from offering their opinion. Again, the prevailing attitudes and behaviors we function with reveal our operating system. And everyone has an operating system. Sadly, most are unaware of what theirs is. Without knowing our operating system, the best we can hope for is accidental success in any area of life, never knowing whether our operating system is giving us our desired results.

Take a minute and ask yourself:

1. *What are some key features of the operating system I am currently running?*

2. *What are the internal attitudes and behaviors that are undermining my success?*

3. *Which ones are giving me ideal outcomes?*

Without understanding the real relationship between what we're investing into our lives and what we're getting out of it; how can we hope to make the necessary adjustments to increase our likelihood of success? We need to pay close attention to what operating system we're running. And here's the good news—you can upgrade your operating system!

Whether we are the CEO of a Fortune 500 company or seeking to grow as a salesperson, whether we are trying to be a better parent or even a better friend, we would do well to make sure we have an operating system that will empower the best version of ourselves for any of these contexts. We need an operating system that will enable us in any situation, at any time, amid any hardships, to optimize proactive and beneficial impact.

I'm going to let you in on a little secret. The empowered life we're all searching for is available when we upgrade our operating system. This is the secret to unlocking our leadership potential. No matter where you find yourself today, the future you long for is waiting on the other side of your willingness to transform how you see yourself, how you interpret the world around you, and how you respond.

Upgrade your attitudes and behaviors if you want to upgrade your life

Make no mistake, we can blame the world for why we aren't getting what we want from life, but the real culprit is our prevailing attitudes and behaviors. It may not be as direct as the input and output relationship of a computer program, but more often than not, we are getting out of life what we are investing into it. Listen carefully: Upgrade your attitudes and behaviors if you want to upgrade your life and leadership.

Shared Operating System = Shared Playbook

Companies use an integrated, shared business system, and our teams need the same. Within any team or organization, a shared

Leadership Operating System acts very much like a team playbook. When team members are all playing from different playbooks, we'll experience breakdowns in communication and execution. Collaborative efforts, decision-making, and problem-solving become more like obstacles than opportunities. Why? Because we're all functioning from different playbooks. This means we all think we know the best way to engage and solve the problems at hand. But who's to say who's right? If a leader does not establish a shared operating system (or playbook), then everyone defaults to their preferences and miscommunication is guaranteed.

You can put all the best athletes on the court, field, or ice, but if they're all playing their own game, they will not perform well together. For this reason, coaches spend lots of time at the beginning of each season introducing their teams to their shared playbook. Their common refrain is, "This is how *we* do it." A team only unlocks its potential when they subscribe to and commit to a shared way of behaving together. And sadly, it only takes one or two team members who decide they know better to derail team performance.

Recently, I sat with a new client over lunch. Charlie is the CEO of a very successful startup whose team was growing faster than he expected. He lamented to me over lunch, "Eric, I've tried to apply so many of the leadership principles I've learned from books and podcasts, but they're not moving the needle. I feel like I'm constantly herding cats!" Charlie had started a recruiting and staffing agency years earlier and experienced unexpected growth. Every new team member represented more work for Charlie as he navigated their inexperience and in-office power struggles. He continued, "I'm spending more time babysitting than doing my job as CEO." I sat there for a moment, remembering my first experiences leading a team and gently shared, "Listen, Charlie, you've built a great company from scratch. But with growth, you've had to add quite a few people to your team, and that's where your greatest challenges are stemming from—people learning how to work well together. This is true for every company. This may feel unfair, but the growth you want to see in your company begins with recognizing that everyone on your team is functioning with different expectations and parameters. In the same way that you don't run multiple operating systems on your devices, your team members need a shared playbook that empowers them individually and collectively."

He immediately shot back, "Didn't you hear what I said? I've tried to do all the things I've read in those leadership books, but they don't work!" A look of shock and anger flashed across Charlie's face. "Eric, I'm doing everything I can to make this team work, but I'm all out of ideas."

I took time to explain to Charlie that knowing lots of good leadership ideas is great, but knowing how to integrate them into his business is what he's looking for. We discussed the need for a shared set of attitudes and behaviors that would help each individual function more effectively, as well as provide an integrated and cohesive playbook to empower team unity and synergy. Then I shared with him the hardest news of all, "Charlie, teams go where their leaders go. You have to decide whether you are ready to upgrade your own leadership before you can ask your team to upgrade theirs. Where the leader goes, so goes the team. The

We simply cannot have teams where everyone is functioning from different playbooks.

change you want to see in your team starts with you. You can own the responsibility of creating the leadership culture you want or avoid it until this blows up in your face." Charlie sat still for a few moments and then conceded, "Ok, explain what you mean."

My lunch with Charlie was similar to so many conversations I've had with leaders who wake up to the reality that everyone on their team is operating from different playbooks. It's even more frustrating when leaders realize that clever vision, mission, or value statements are not the fix. Once leaders recognize the radical importance of establishing a shared leadership system for their teams, synergy and collaboration are inevitable. When they see where the chaos stems from, it becomes painfully clear what the solution is. We simply cannot have teams where everyone is functioning from different playbooks. Once teams begin to implement a shared way of behaving, they experience the joy of working together more efficiently and effectively. This leads to greater satisfaction and results.

Be a Charlie, Not a Bob

People really are the engine of any team or organization. How they operate individually and collectively determines their ability to reduce unnecessary friction and engage their work with greater enjoyment. Implementing a shared playbook is the only valid solution to the problem of team dysfunction, toxicity, turnover and fragmentation. Whether you're working with a small team or with hundreds, people cannot effectively work together when operating from different playbooks.

Sadly, Bob could not accept this reality. Even after committing many months to working with Bob, he determined he was an old dog and could not learn new tricks. Charlie, on the other hand, determined he would take on the responsibility of providing his team with a shared playbook. In a very short period of time, his team began to see the results they were looking for. Speed of communication increased, while gossip and triangulation had all but disappeared. Now, Charlie spends less time navigating internal frustrations and more time focused on building his business. His team now operates with greater synchronicity and purpose.

The leader you want to become and the future you're desiring *are* on the other side of upgrading your operating system. You can become a valuable leader in any context and have a competitive advantage over those who don't do the work. Your team and organization can achieve immeasurably more than you can even imagine. The only question is, are you ready to upgrade your operating system? Are you ready to be a Charlie, not a Bob?

TAKEAWAYS

- The vast majority of leaders were not trained for their leadership responsibilities.
- Talent doesn't compensate for character.
- An individual is never more important than the team or business.
- Every person has developed their own way of operating from their earliest years
- Each of us can become better leaders by upgrading how we operate

REFLECTION QUESTIONS

- What's one default behavior in your leadership that may no longer serve you?
- What early life experience or belief might have shaped the way you operate under pressure today?

02

WE NEED A LEADERSHIP OPERATING SYSTEM

If we want to optimize our performance and that of our teams, we must upgrade our leadership. We need an operating system that provides two basic functions: 1) To lead ourselves, which is to bring the best version of ourselves to any situation, and 2) To lead others so they are empowered. Leading ourselves well and leading others well is the key that unlocks our potential and the potential of those around us. We call this a Leadership Operating System (LOS).

In the beginning, our clients often lament that their teams are not operating with the core leadership skills necessary to thrive under pressure. As we process the gaps in their performance, they quickly agree they need to upgrade their functionality, and their team needs the same. For this reason, we help them upgrade to an LOS, which includes the necessary tools, skills and integration of empowered leadership practices to optimize both individual and collaborative performance.

Remember, everyone has an individual operating system, but **not everyone has a Leadership Operating System.**

Remember, everyone has an individual operating system, but not everyone has a Leadership Operating System. For those who upgrade to an LOS, they experience a competitive advantage over those who have not. Their ability to operate with composure in high pressure situations, to build unified and resilient teams, and to collaborate with others toward ambitious goals sets them apart. These are the leaders who operate with a growth mindset and achieve more than anyone thought possible. Our LOS ensures that leaders and teams realize more of their potential.

Why? Because they know how to effectively lead themselves and others when it matters most!

WHY the LOS Works!

In the same way that software engineers can rewrite the code for any program to upgrade its operating capacity, we can rewrite our personal operating system to ensure we're functioning in a way that unlocks our ability to engage all our responsibilities with greater ease and confidence. Thankfully, we don't need to understand computer coding, algorithms, or programs to rewrite and upgrade our own operating systems. So, what do we need to know?

Before we turn our attention the core leadership tools that will transform how we function, it's vital that we understand why and how these tools are so incredibly empowering.

Timeless Principles - The LOS Toolkit is based on leadership principles that have served humanity for generations and across all cultures. Because these tools are rooted in universal human principles, they're easily adopted by anyone. To date, I haven't worked with a single leader who found any of the tools incompatible with their personal values, cultural traditions, or religious beliefs. In fact, I always encourage new clients to test the tools. If they find that any principle is incompatible with the kind of leader they want to be, they are free to dismiss it. I simply tell them, "These tools must represent the kind of leader you want to be and the culture you want to create—or you need to find a different LOS." So far, after investing this LOS in hundreds of leaders across various industries, there have been no compatibility issues.

Accessible & Adaptable - A question I get a lot is, "Will this LOS translate into our company, industry or context?" I like to answer this with a question: "Is your company run by human beings?" The reply is always an awkward, "Yes." I follow up with, "Then this LOS will work for you and your team."

I heard an executive lament, "Building a business would be so much easier if it weren't for all the people!" We can all sympathize with that. Relationships in any context are challenging, and when everyone operates from a different operating system, the difficulties multiply. Our LOS doesn't promise to eliminate all the challenges of working with people, but it does promise to make navigating those challenges more efficient, leading to greater outcomes.

Our goal isn't to solve all your problems for you—it's to equip you with the skills to solve them yourself. Leadership isn't about having all the answers. It's about harnessing the collective genius in any group to solve problems and adapt amidst challenges and unexpected circumstances. Our efforts as leaders are easily undermined when people operate with incompatible operating systems. Remember, you can't run two different operating systems on the same device!

Leadership isn't about having all the answers. It's about harnessing the collective genius in any group to solve problems and adapt amidst challenges and unexpected circumstances.

Simple, Visual Tools - As humans we crave visual recognition. We know Disneyland by the three circles that make up Mickey Mouse's head and we know Starbucks by the circular green siren that is plastered on cups, buildings and all marketing. We know McDonalds by the yellow arches, and we recognize Amazon by the smiley face underscoring their name. Our brains are wired to recognize good and bad by virtue of what we see, therefore we have developed visual leadership tools that encompass the timeless and transcendent principles and practices we all long for.

Of course I'm not the genius who created these leadership principles, but I learned from a former mentor that we need to constantly "innovate on the greatest ideas from the past, otherwise we forget who we are." Our LOS is comprised of the hallmark leadership principles and practices that have empowered the greatest leaders throughout history.

The advantage of visual tools is that they're simple, memorable, transferable, and therefore scalable. You can easily illustrate them on the back of a napkin or throw them on a whiteboard. If you can draw a circle, square, or line, then you can draw any of our tools.

Memorable - As our LOS is based on eight visual tools, it means they are more memorable. Because our brains are able to recall the principles and practices of these visual tools, it is more likely we will practice them. We can all relate to particular disciplines we learned in the past, whether it be playing an instrument, riding a bike or learning a new software program. If what we learned is memorable, it is more likely we can reproduce this skill when the situation calls for it.

Easily Transferable - If we can remember *what* we have learned and *how* we learned it, then we can share it with others. This is the basis for reproducing our knowledge and know-how with others. I first became intrigued with visual leadership tools because after reading a great number of leadership books, I could only remember those ideas that were connected to visual images. From there, I realized that I could share what I had learned with others by sharing the relevant

> The greatest tragedy is **learning something that has transformed your life that you can't share with someone else.**

visual image on a napkin or piece of paper. The greatest tragedy is learning something that has transformed your life that you can't share with someone else.

Interestingly, in working with leaders from a variety of backgrounds, their common complaint is related to having learned something in an academic context they cannot translate into a real work environment. Perhaps you were able to join an MBA program or some other advanced leadership training. If you cannot translate what you have learned to those you lead, what you have learned is of no real advantage. In fact, this perpetuates the misnomer that only those with particular degrees can lead well.

Scalable Impact - We all want scalable impact. From our homes to our workplace, all of us want to believe that we can change the culture of our environment. Our LOS is uniquely designed to provide all the features that ensure scalability: timeless principles, universal accessibility, and visual, memorable tools that can be transferred from one person to the next.

Scalability ensures us that what works for one person also works for tens, hundreds and thousands of others. Our toolkit is designed so that anyone can upgrade and optimize their overall performance.

A Playbook – Shared Tools, Language & Practices

When we upgrade our teams to an LOS, we can enjoy the benefits of having shared tools, shared language and shared practices. Our LOS provides leaders and teams with clear operating protocols for how we:

- respond to challenges
- resolve conflict
- make timely decisions
- foster unity
- leverage the collective genius, and so much more.

Every leader wants to build a championship-caliber culture, and for this, you must know how to get everyone to play from the same playbook.

Shared Tools - The leadership toolkit provides a structured framework to clarify expectations and boundaries for how we can operate really well, especially under difficult circumstances. One tool shows us how to operate from a posture of personal responsibility, while another tool provides a pathway to create a culture of trust and resilience. Some tools work together to ensure we have a pipeline of ready and available team members. Other tools work together so we can handle any problem with sober engagement (which leads to better outcomes). If we're all committed to operating with the same *playbook*, then we're all accountable to the same system of attitudes and behaviors.

In a recent session with an executive team, the CFO openly challenged the CEO on the basis that he wasn't filtering the problem at hand through the shared toolkit. The CEO thanked his teammate and used the moment as an opportunity to reaffirm his commitment to operating in a consistent, predictable manner. The LOS has radically transformed this team's ability to handle the daily fires with greater composure and courage. Instead of fighting each other, they are now fighting together to work through challenges and continuously course correct.

Shared Language - The LOS Toolkit found in this book also provides shared language, which expedites communication, allowing everyone to get on the same page more readily.

An owner-operator of a mid-sized technology company shared a story of how one of their teams had sorely underestimated the timeline for the production of a critical component, which resulted in not being able to deliver their technology to their clients as promised. They gathered the relevant leaders, and the meeting began with everyone blaming the other. After some time, someone in the meeting broke in with, "Isn't this just another 'Kairos moment?' What if we slowed down, each took 100 percent responsibility for their part in this challenge and we worked together to solve the problem?" Everyone in the meeting nodded their heads and immediately chose to align themselves with their shared LOS. The shared language became a catalyst to get everyone rowing in the same direction again. (We'll learn what a "Kairos moment" is later!)

Shared Practices - The LOS Toolkit provides shared expectations and shared practices to ensure that leaders and teams function in the best interest of all parties involved. I remember being in a conflict engagement training session with a team, when an older man casually said to me, "I love conflict and have no problem doing it!" The only problem is that his way of engaging in conflict included yelling, name-calling, and belittling the other party until they surrendered to his view. Understanding the value of conflict and hard conversations is one thing but doing it well is another.

One of our tools provides a six-step process for solving problems, making decisions and resolving conflict. If everyone agrees on how we do these things, then we're more likely to come out on the other side with the desired results. Remember, differing operating systems usually lead to chaos and irreparable damage, especially in relationships.

It bears repeating: How your people operate, individually and collectively, determines the power and performance of your business. If they can function in sync, even when faced with battles, they'll certainly come out on top!

HOW the LOS Works!

One of the key responsibilities for leaders at any level, in any context, is to identify and solve problems. I constantly have to remind my clients: the greater your responsibility, the more that is at stake. It is critical to solve problems successfully.

The function of the LOS Toolkit is to provide you with a framework of interpretive lenses that will help you see problems quickly, interpret them accurately, and respond effectively.

Individually, each tool serves us in a variety of key leadership challenges. Collectively, the toolkit gives us the needed peace of mind and confidence to tackle whatever comes our way to ensure the best possible outcomes. Here's how:

The LOS provides for us a clear vision for the kind of culture we want to create.

Vision for your culture - We must have a clear vision of how we expect ourselves and others to operate in any team environment. When I ask clients to describe the kind of leader they want to be or what they want the prevailing attitudes and behaviors of their team to be, they usually stare back at me like deer in headlights. They may offer some thoughts, but no clear vision for what they want in their leadership culture.

The LOS we're about to explore will provide you with a clear vision for the kind of leader you want to be as well as the quality of culture worth fighting for in any context.

Diagnostic Lenses - Leaders rarely ever call me in to help them identify their tension points; they already know them. They invite me in to help them understand where the frustrations are coming from and how to transform their pain into progress. Our coaching business goes a step further. We train leaders with our LOS, so they have the specific interpretive lenses to understand and resolve their own problems.

We don't want leaders and organizations to be dependent on our coaching services indefinitely. Therefore, we ensure they are trained, equipped, and confident to do for themselves what we do for them in the beginning. The best leaders are coaching leaders— leaders who can coach themselves and others into greater alignment with their LOS.

Practical Handles to Move the Needle - The LOS will also empower you to leverage the collective genius of your community to discover the best way forward in any situation. As leadership coaches, it is not our job to tell our clients what to do, but instead to help them discover for themselves the best way forward. We teach them to harness the intelligence, creativity and experience of those around them to make great decisions and execute with courage. The LOS Toolkit will dramatically increase your confidence to lead through any challenge, knowing how to transform any obstacle into an opportunity for growth, development and greater success.

From Player to NBA General Manager: Landry Fields

I've had the privilege of working with Landry Fields during his rocket-like ascension from professional player to NBA General Manager. We met at a friend's birthday party, where we connected over a shared passion for personal and leadership development.

At the time, he was a scout for the San Antonio Spurs and shared his desire to optimize his own leadership intelligence. His humility, growth mindset, and work ethic indicated he would be an ideal candidate for our executive coaching process. In a very short period, Landry eagerly learned the LOS Toolkit and upgraded his leadership capacity.

He was eventually recruited by the Atlanta Hawks, who recognized their own need for a leadership upgrade. Though Landry was understandably nervous about this new opportunity, we agreed the only way to know how much he'd grown is to put it to the test. He accepted their offer and moved his family to a new city.

Very quickly, Landry became aware that many of his new colleagues were operating from different playbooks. Up to that point, the front office had been more focused on winning games than their leadership culture. Departments were siloed, ideas rarely made their way up-chain, and most were afraid to take risks for fear of losing their jobs. The program was underperforming, and the disempowering culture in the front office was reflected in the team's on-court play.

It was a heavy lift, but Landry began the slow, painstaking work of introducing the organization to the MPWR Leadership Operating System. Slowly, but surely, team members started owning their part in the organization's culture and committing themselves to getting better each day. Toxic personalities found it difficult to stay in an environment that was focused on open, honest communication. Today, if you have the privilege of spending time at their facility, you'll encounter a group of talented individuals who find great joy in working together, pushing one another toward greater heights, and believing that a championship-caliber program is possible when they're all rowing in the same direction.

Many have asked how someone so young could rise so quickly in a star-studded industry where others have spent decades without reaching the same status. I believe Landry's opportunities are directly proportional to the work he has done on himself. He may not have the same experience as other GMs in the league, but his insatiable desire for growth and transformation marks him as someone whose leadership trajectory is always on the rise. Not only that, he expects everyone around him to be on a constant growth journey. He calls this Kairos-Kaizen—a mindset that regularly identifies opportunities for continual improvement. After working with this organization for a few years, I can say they have created a leadership culture where everyone brings not only the best of their skills and abilities, but also a high quality of character, chemistry, and team unity.

Landry's leadership philosophy cannot guarantee an NBA Championship, or even a certain record of wins and losses, but it can guarantee that their program will harness the collective genius of all team members to unlock the program's potential. What if we were less obsessed with short-term results (most of which we cannot control) and instead focused on unlocking our potential? Our team's potential? Our organization's potential?

As they say, shoot for the stars and you may reach the moon. Great leaders understand their responsibility is to help their team

Great leaders understand their responsibility is to help their team and organization optimize their performance, which invariably produces greater results over time.

and organization optimize their performance, which invariably produces greater results over time. Focus on optimization, and you get results. Focus solely on results, and you'll miss the opportunities for optimization.

Landry is a reminder that leaders are responsible for creating a culture that drives increasing and sustainable results! The future of business will be owned by those who prioritize long-term success over short-term gain.

TAKEAWAYS

- If we want to optimize our performance and that of our teams, we must upgrade our operating system.
- Everyone has an *individual* operating system, but not everyone has a *leadership* operating system.
- This LOS is based on eight visual tools, making it memorable and easily transferable.

REFLECTION QUESTIONS

- Can you remember an occasion in your organization where one or more people were utilizing their *individual* operating systems, creating conflict or issues?
- How might things have been different if there had been a simple, repeatable framework for people to follow, instead of their own default systems?

03

CULTURES THAT DRIVE SUSTAINABLE RESULTS

Think of the different roles in your team or company as applications on a device. Each person has unique responsibilities, much like an app is designed to solve a specific problem. Just as a device can run thousands of apps, the LOS ensures that people in different roles fulfill their duties effectively, in alignment with one another, and within the company's vision.

No matter the specific role, every team member must be able to:

- Communicate
- Make decisions
- Engage in conflict
- Learn
- Grow
- Solve problems.

They must do all of this daily, and under pressure. Yet, while most companies clarify *what* employees should be doing, very few pay attention to *how* people do what they do. This neglect is why HR departments are often overwhelmed by complaints about behaviors like gossip, unresolved conflicts, passive-aggressive tendencies and so on. Too often, team members are removed, not because they're lacking work-related skills, but because they're toxic to their environment. The *how* undermines the *what* every day.

The **how** undermines the **what** every day.

Most leaders don't understand that the prevailing attitudes and behaviors of a group creates culture, and most feel ill-equipped to identify and change the culture. Let's make sure you're not one of those folks! Culture can be easily understood through the chorus of a well-known song by Montell Jordan, "This Is How We Do It." If you know the tune, hum it to yourself and you'll never forget what culture is. "This is how we do it!"

No matter the value statements on your website or office walls, the default attitudes and behaviors of your team create your actual culture. And when there is a disconnect between your aspirational values (as stated on a document) and your practiced values (as reflected in prevailing behaviors), it robs your team or company of its integrity and your people-engine sputters.

As leaders, it is our responsibility to clarify our expectations, both for *what* we want from our team members as well as *how* we expect them to operate individually and collectively. Unless we're providing this clarity, we cannot hold them accountable for growth, development and outcomes. When we align our cultural expectations with clear behavioral standards, we experience the synergy that comes from the intersection between *what* we do and *how* we do it.

Alignment Begins with Clear Standards

The LOS found in this book is designed to align how people lead and work, ensuring that everyone—from top executives to frontline employees—operates according to clear standards. This sets baseline expectations for both performance and behavior, creating a shared understanding of how success is achieved and maintained. Without it, people default to their own methods, leading to confusion, misalignment, and ultimately, failure.

Let me share a story to illustrate. Jenna, a regional manager for a growing retail chain, was frustrated with her store managers. Some were hitting sales targets but creating toxic work environments, while others fostered great cultures but couldn't seem to drive revenue. The inconsistency was causing chaos across their region. Jenna realized they were all operating with different personal standards for leadership, which led to unpredictable results. After implementing our LOS, she introduced clear standards for behavior and execution: Every store would focus on both hard metrics, like sales targets, and soft metrics, like employee satisfaction.

She also clarified how each manager was expected to lead, setting clear standards for communication, conflict resolution, and decision-making.

Within months, the stores had transformed. The managers were no longer competing on separate tracks; they were united in how they led and what they were working toward. By aligning their behaviors with clear standards, the entire region became more consistent, and success followed. Jenna realized it wasn't just about the results—it was about *how* those results were achieved, and the LOS gave her the framework to ensure both were in harmony.

The purpose of the LOS is simple: to drive a Radical Minimum Standard for leadership engagement across your organization, ensuring that everyone operates from the same playbook. It's the difference between teams that function in silos and those that thrive together, pushing the boundaries of what's possible. With a clear LOS driving clear expectations, you'll see greater success because your team isn't just working hard—they're working smarter together.

Leaders Provide Clear Standards

The Radical Minimum Standard Diagram illustrates the key components necessary to ensure our teams are clear on three things:

1. What's expected of them

2. Opportunities for growth

3. How accountability plays a critical role in optimizing performance.

This diagram applies whether you're leading a Fortune 500 company, coaching a youth sports team, shaping your household's dynamics, or pushing yourself to new heights in personal performance.

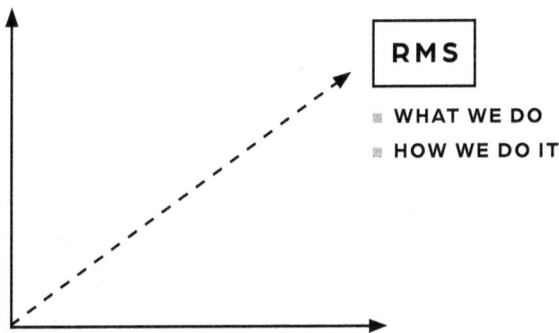

Our job as leaders is to clarify the RMS—what the group is fighting for—through the lens of both *what* we do and *how* we do it. Whether it's quarterly sales targets, the opening and closing procedures for a restaurant, how we make decisions, resolve conflict, or the number of wins needed to make the playoffs—setting clear expectations around what we're trying to achieve is critical. Without this clarity, how can we ever know if we're winning?

THE WHAT – Job Specific Skills

In any space, there will be industry or context-specific competencies people need to achieve in order to execute their roles and responsibilities. These expectations must be clear and communicated upfront, so everyone knows exactly what they're accountable for. This is usually communicated in the form of job roles and responsibilities. For instance, how many calls or follow-ups we expect from our sales team or what "clean your room" means for my son (as I quickly learned in parenting!). If we don't clarify these expectations, people will default to what *they* think is sufficient, and that inevitably leads to frustration on all sides.

THE HOW – Attitudes and Behaviors

This might sound basic, but leaders often assume their teams will naturally operate with the right attitudes and behaviors. And yet, very quickly, we discover the gap between who we *thought* we hired and who actually shows up a few months down the road. That's why it's crucial to clarify *how* we expect people to behave. These are often referred to as soft skills, but I assure you they are critical for achieving sustained success. I frequently remind leaders that a lack of social skills undermines even the most brilliant and competent people on our team. In short, if we don't develop the soft skills needed for effective leadership, it won't matter how great someone's hard skills are.

Most systemic problems in organizations don't arise from a lack of technical understanding, but from insubordination, disengagement, or combative behaviors. Even when working with highly educated adults, we can't assume they'll know how to function well within a team environment.

While many leaders focus on what needs to get done, don't forget that how we operate shapes the culture. Attention to the *how* will pay significant dividends toward your overall success. Time and again, my company is called in to solve the *what* (problems, missed goals, underperformance), but we consistently find the root cause to be in *how* people are operating individually and collectively.

> Culture is simply **how** we do **what** we do.

Remember, "This is how we do it."

That phrase is culture in a nutshell. Culture is simply *how* we do *what* we do. Clarifying and reinforcing the *how* is a surefire way to create or reshape culture. Of course, the pressures of meeting deadlines and making sales calls tempts us to prioritize our output, but the LOS Toolkit found in this book has the power to align your culture for greater output.

Assessing our Team

Now, let's take a minute to unpack the two axis that make up the RMS Diagram.

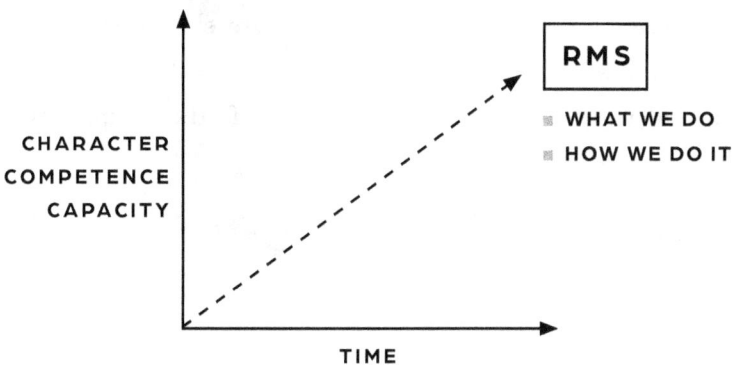

When hiring new team members or evaluating current ones, there are three key areas we must always assess, and they should factor into how we clarify expectations:

Character - Character is often the hardest to screen for during hiring, but it's essential. Character is measured through honesty, humility, dependability and responsibility. We should always contact former employers and ask questions that dig into how a candidate handled difficulties. With so much of our lives online, it's worth doing some light research in that area. Ask interview questions designed to reveal self-awareness, which is usually a great indicator of good character. I always tell clients: we hire for skill but often end up firing for lack of character. It's worth the effort to screen for the qualities of character that align with our standards.

We'll dive deeper into the issue of character in a later chapter, but for now let's remember character is largely responsible for whether people grow or plateau.

Competence - This is where most companies focus when hiring, but we need to go beyond just job-specific skills. Competence should also include the leadership skills necessary to operate effectively within your organization. These skills include communication, conflict engagement, problem-solving, learning, self-leadership, and more. If we don't clarify these expectations

Character is largely responsible for whether people grow or plateau.

upfront, how can we hold people accountable for creating the culture we want?

Capacity - Capacity refers to someone's mental, emotional, and physical bandwidth. It is crucial to assess this throughout someone's journey in your company because their capacity directly impacts their ability to meet our expectations. While probing into someone's personal life can be tricky for legal reasons, we must stay attuned to indicators of whether someone has the bandwidth to handle the responsibilities expected of them. Factors like health, family issues, and even commuting distances can impact capacity.

Let's pay attention to the diagram's upward vector (RMS line), signifying that growth and development are baked into the company's culture. "What got you here won't get you there." The principles of this diagram reflect a simple yet powerful way to ensure that individuals, teams, and organizations continue to grow and evolve in their capacity.

Accountability for Growth

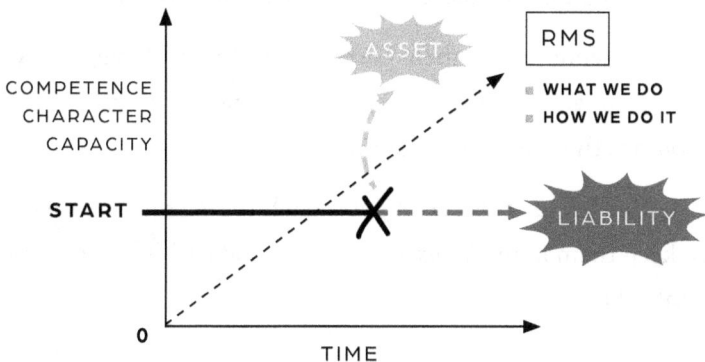

1. As important as it is to clarify standards and expectations for those we lead, we must also maintain a culture of accountability. Assuming we've done our best to clarify and communicate a Radical Minimum Standard (RMS), consider the following:

2. Every employee starts (at 0 time) a new position above the RMS, or they wouldn't have been hired in the first place. It is expected that everyone will fall below the RMS at some point (illustrated by the X below the RMS line). This is called being human - we're all a work in progress! Falling below the RMS simply exposes a potential growth area. The leader's responsibility is to help the individual identify how they're operating below the RMS and give them an opportunity to raise their performance (*what* & *how*) to, or above, the RMS. Many companies address this process with a performance plan.

3. If someone persists below the RMS, they are operating as a LIABILITY to the team or organization. In this case we must determine whether they should be given more time, moved to a different role, or transitioned out of the organization.

If someone raises their performance to, or above, the RMS, they are operating as an ASSET. They should be celebrated to encourage their progress into the future.

I often tell my team what got them hired isn't necessarily what will keep them here. We expect growth, and we build accountability into that journey.

Recalibrating Your Standards & Expectations

As leaders, we'll discover from time to time our RMS is unclear or we haven't communicated often enough. We may also discover our standards need to be adjusted because they are either too high or low. This is to be expected and affords us an opportunity to practice what we're asking of those around us, to be flexible, to learn and to make necessary changes. Our RMS will often require recalibration as we discover a better way to set expectations. This is normal. The important thing isn't that we get it right the first time, but that we're committed to shifting our standards to serve others and our environment best.

Dana is a customer support manager for a tech company and offers a great illustration of the importance of aligning our standards with our LOS. She established a new RMS, requiring team members to respond to every customer inquiry within one hour. Her team's LOS prioritized responsiveness, empathy, and efficient problem-solving, and she believed this new RMS would enhance customer satisfaction.

However, as the team began to feel the strain of keeping up with this rapid response time, Dana noticed quality dipping. Responses were rushed, and team members were losing morale. Dana realized that her RMS might be pushing the team too hard without delivering the desired results.

Dana initiated a team conversation focused on adjusting the response standard. They decided to set a more realistic expectation: urgent inquiries would still receive a one-hour response, but other queries would have a three-hour window to ensure thoughtful replies. Dana's willingness to recalibrate the RMS based on their operational values helped the team refocus on empathy and problem-solving. As a result, the team's morale improved, customer satisfaction rose, and Dana demonstrated that a flexible RMS, grounded in their LOS, could sustain high standards without sacrificing team well-being.

As leaders, we get to create a culture where every success and failure is another opportunity for leadership development. Our people will be more likely to own their own failures and embrace the sometimes-painful journey toward growth if we set an expectation for personal and professional transformation from the beginning. I often share with my team that I expect they will be a better version of themselves when they depart from my company than when they first entered. Leading in this way will help everyone integrate their *what* and *how*, which leads to more healthy and productive teams.

TAKEAWAYS

- Too often, team members are removed, not because they're lacking work-related skills, but because they're toxic to their environment.

- When hiring new team members or evaluating current ones, we must always assess character, competence and capacity.

- Culture is simply *how* we do *what* we do.

- The RMS (Radical Minimum Standard) diagram will help define expectations and track growth.

REFLECTIVE QUESTIONS

- Have you set a clear RMS for the team you're leading?

- What does accountability for your team look like? Is it effective to encourage growth?

- Are you embodying your RMS and leading by example?

04

THE CHANGE YOU'RE LOOKING FOR STARTS WITH YOU

In the first three chapters, we discussed how upgrading your Leadership Operating System (LOS) empowers you to lead more effectively and build a winning culture. In the next section we'll have a chance to upgrade our operating system and unlock more of our potential, but first we must address the one thing that will sabotage our journey. Yes, that's right...the greatest enemy to our leadership is *ourselves*.

Leadership isn't just about managing others—it starts with managing yourself. Every day, we're faced with triggers that can knock us off course, and how we handle these moments directly impacts our performance as leaders. This is where the LOS Toolkit comes into play, offering practical tools to help you recognize and manage these triggers, equipping you to stay on track and operate with clarity and resilience.

> The cornerstone of confident, resilient leadership lies in **taking 100 percent responsibility for our attitudes and behaviors.**

In the following chapters, we'll dive into the LOS Toolkit, but first, let's address the real enemy of our leadership. Surprisingly, it's not other people; it's what happens inside us when the pressure mounts. Under stress, we can become our own worst enemies, holding ourselves back from bringing the best version of ourselves to any situation. The cornerstone of confident, resilient leadership lies in taking 100 percent responsibility for our attitudes and behaviors, instead of shifting blame to the world around us.

The Power of Personal Responsibility

We all get triggered. To be human is to get triggered. In fact, most of us feel triggered multiple times each day. Maybe it's an unwelcome text or email. Perhaps it's a coworker's unsavory sense of humor. Or it might just be that the barista put a little too much milk in your iced coffee. We all feel triggered by experiences that don't line up with our expectations or preferences. Often, we're able to cope with these triggers and muscle through the day, but oftentimes they catch up to us. Have you ever gotten to the end of a day feeling like you barely survived it? Yep, join the party. Navigating triggers is part of our daily lives.

In leadership, triggers can be anything from a difficult customer to a tense conversation with a colleague. If we don't manage these reactions, they can sabotage our decision-making, strain relationships, and prevent us from leading with clarity and confidence. Recognizing and managing triggers is a critical skill in maintaining leadership composure and influence.

A trigger is any experience that impacts us mentally, emotionally, and physically. Humans are integrated beings, which means when we are impacted in one of these areas, it almost always affects the others. Try stubbing your toe without your mind and emotions following suit. Or think of the last time someone shot a biting comment your way. I'll bet your emotions flared, your heart raced a little, and your mind flooded with thoughts of shock or retribution.

Every negative trigger poses a threat to our well-being, or at least that's how we feel. Many of us have well-worn coping mechanisms, but everyone has a breaking point. When a big enough trigger hits, or many smaller ones pile up, we eventually hit our limit and find ourselves saying or doing things we later regret. This is called getting hijacked.

When we're hijacked by a trigger, we lose the ability to lead with clarity. In these moments, our reactions undermine our ability to make sound decisions, resolve conflicts constructively, and inspire others. We move into a self-protecting posture and give way to various expressions of fight, flight, or fold. Moreover, if we can't recover from the flood of hijacked thoughts, emotions, and physical sensations, we find ourselves pinballing—like a pinball in a machine—bouncing from one trigger to the next, desperately trying to stay out of the gutter.

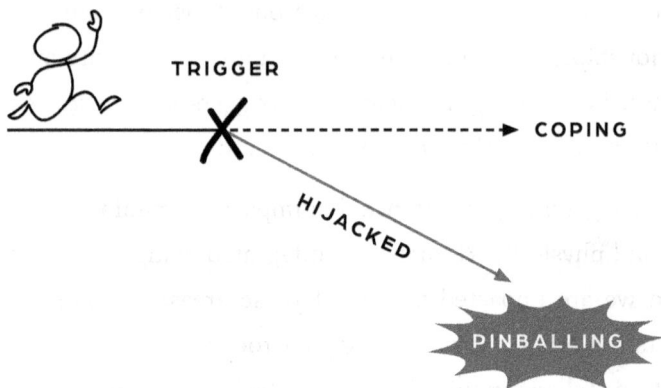

Recognize that the difference between the best version of you and the worst in these moments is a matter of choice. The greatest power every person has is their ability to choose how they engage even the most challenging experiences.

Of course, it's easier to blame the world around us for why we're operating with bad attitudes and behaviors, but how's that working for you? Blaming others for our poor behavior is like blaming the sun for a sunburn after spending hours outside without sunblock. Getting out of bed each day will expose you to triggers—that's inevitable. How you respond is within your power, and to think differently is self-deception.

We don't get to choose whether we are triggered, but we do get to choose how we respond. *This is our superpower.* The next diagram reveals that at the point of every hijacking, there is an opportunity to take a different pathway. We call this the pathway of personal responsibility. Personal responsibility requires that we reject the temptations of a victim or villain mindset, where we view the world as happening *to* us. It invites us to understand that while we cannot control the world, we are 100 percent responsible for our attitudes and behaviors at all times.

Practicing personal responsibility gives us back our power. We realize we're not victims of our experiences but beneficiaries. We wake up to the fact that life is happening *for* us, not *to* us. This upward trajectory leads to increased composure, clarity, confidence, and courage. Instead of waiting for the next shoe to drop, we tackle life with conviction, knowing we get to make of life whatever we choose.

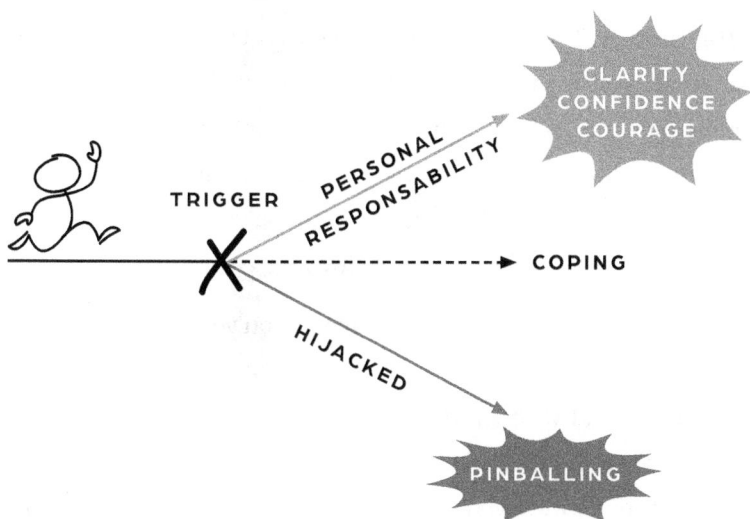

Now, the only thing standing in your way is you. You get to choose whether you want to spend more time on the upward trajectory than the downward one. The more we practice the skills of personal responsibility, the faster our recovery rate.

Disrupting Ourselves

There are two questions we can ask ourselves when triggered and hijacked that will disrupt our familiar defaults and give us the best chance of choosing the pathway of personal responsibility:

1. What does the best version of me look like in responding to this situation?

2. What does it look like for me to take 100 percent responsibility for my part in this situation?

In the beginning, we'll likely only realize we've been hijacked after the fact. That's ok. But once we recognize it, we get to choose whether to stay on the lower trajectory or change direction and move onto the upward trajectory by disrupting old patterns and asking the above questions. The time it takes us to realize where we are and choose a better version of ourselves is called our recovery rate (as seen in the diagram below).

The faster you can recognize when you've been hijacked and return to the best version of yourself, the more consistently you'll be able to lead with confidence and composure. In the diagram below, we see how simple (albeit, not easy) it is to move from the lower to the upward trajectory. Welcome to the world of continuous personal growth and performance optimization!

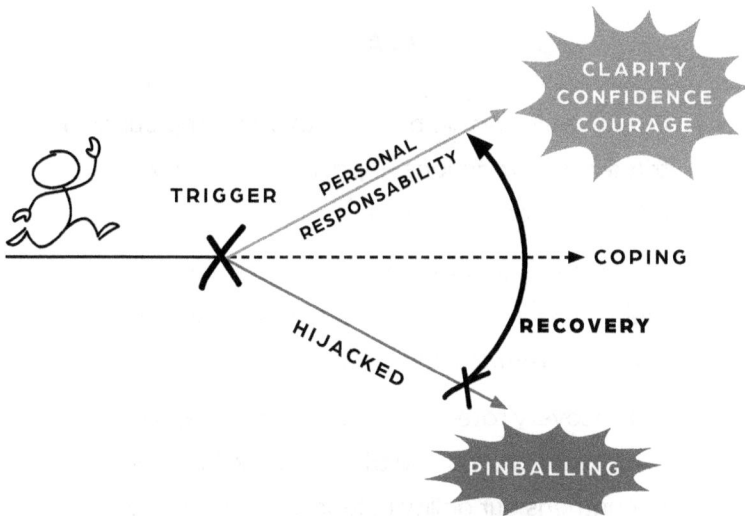

Optimizing our performance is the purpose of this book. So far, we have set the stage for what we're fighting for, why it matters, and what gets in the way. To unlock our full potential, we now must do the hard work of upgrading our operating system to a Leadership Operating System. This LOS will give you the ability to become the best leader of yourself and others. You'll unlock a greater degree of your intelligence, emotional and relational agility, and become the kind of leader the world desperately needs.

Mastering the ability to take personal responsibility and manage your triggers is just the beginning. To truly unlock your potential as a leader, you need the right tools. In the next part of this book, we'll introduce our LOS Toolkit—an array of visual tools designed to help you practice personal responsibility, navigate challenges with clarity, empower those around you and lead so others want to follow.

TAKEAWAYS

- Effective leadership begins with managing our own triggers and reactions, impacting our ability to lead others with confidence.

- Choosing personal responsibility over blame is foundational for resilient leadership, giving us control over our attitudes and behaviors.

- Our recovery rate—the time it takes to regain composure after being triggered and hijacked—strengthens our ability to lead consistently and with clarity.

REFLECTION QUESTIONS

- Think about a time when you got triggered and then hijacked. What would it have looked like if you had chosen the pathway of personal responsibility instead? Imagine yourself making that choice.

- Can you remember a time you witnessed someone responding to a trigger in a clear, composed way? What were your thoughts at the time?

PART TWO

LOS: THE LEADERSHIP OPERATING SYSTEM TOOLKIT

05

EQ MATRIX

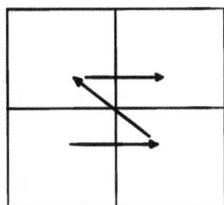

LEADING YOURSELF SO YOU
CAN LEAD OTHERS

E motional intelligence (EQ) is now understood in many circles as the foundation for great leadership. Some have referred to these as a set of soft or touchy-feely skills, yet I can assure you, mastering the skills of emotional intelligence is ridiculously hard. Why? Because it begins and is sustained by mastery of one's *self*. But in order to master oneself, we must be able to clearly see ourselves, and that's easier said than done.

Developing the skills of emotional intelligence as outlined in this chapter is the foundation of our Leadership Operating System (LOS). The framework provided here will illuminate both the kind of leader we aspire to be and the kind of culture that empowers any team and organization. One person operating in alignment with this framework can move the needle in any area substantially. A team operating with this framework can move mountains.

The EQ Matrix

In the EQ Matrix diagram below, we see there are two key relationships we must engage with every day: first, with ourselves, and second, with others. In these two relationships, there are two primary engagements we must pay attention to: awareness and leadership. Interestingly, every life experience can be understood through the lens of these four quadrants and seeing whether or not we operate well in each.

	AWARE	LEAD
OTHERS	OTHERS AWARE	OTHERS LEAD
SELF	SELF AWARE	SELF LEAD

Let me quickly tie this tool to the previous chapter's Personal Responsibility Diagram. When we get triggered, hijacked, or find ourselves pinballing, our natural instinct is to interpret the source of this experience in the upper quadrants of others-awareness and others-leadership. After all, we usually get triggered by other people. However, the practice of emotional intelligence is always an invitation to recognize that our being triggered is an "us" problem, primarily rooted in the lower left quadrant of self-awareness. Remember, only we can be 100 percent responsible for our attitudes and behaviors and how we respond to any experience.

Consider an iceberg. Ninety percent of its mass is hidden beneath the surface. I believe 90 percent of what goes on in our lives is tied to what's happening internally. Sadly, we often find ourselves spending 90 percent of our energy trying to force the world around us to conform to our expectations, focused on what's happening above the waterline, missing the real locus of control— which is ourselves. Greater mastery over our thoughts, emotions, and physical expressions leads to a greater mastery of how we engage others.

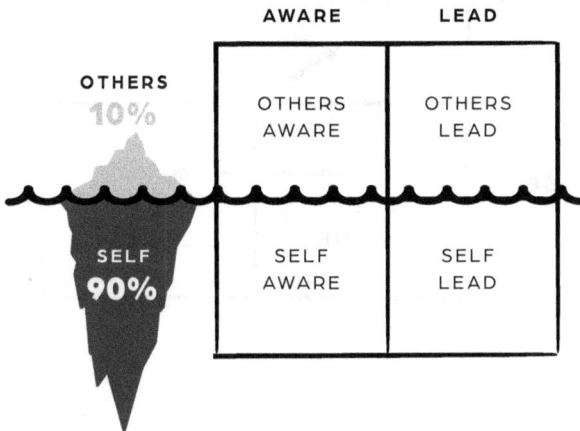

	AWARE	LEAD
OTHERS 10%	OTHERS AWARE	OTHERS LEAD
SELF 90%	SELF AWARE	SELF LEAD

To understand what's at stake, we can only give to others (above the line) what we first cultivate in ourselves (below the line). If we're stewing on anger, hostility, resentment, bitterness, frustration, impatience, or self-doubt, that's what inevitably leaks out in our engagement with others. I have to remind myself and my clients regularly that our attitudes and behaviors always reveal what's going on inside of us, for better and worse. On the other hand, if we are cultivating patience, kindness, self-love, and self-control, that's also what leaks out in how we operate.

As we'll see, each quadrant builds on the previous one and gives us a clear roadmap for practicing the pathway of personal responsibility. Now, let's briefly unpack the core skills for each of these quadrants.

PATHWAY OF PERSONAL RESPONSIBILITY

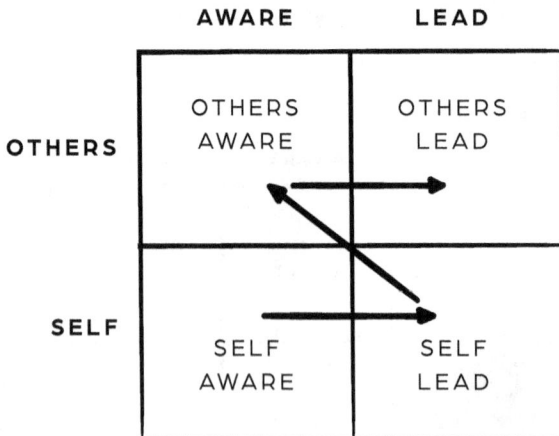

	AWARE	**LEAD**
OTHERS	OTHERS AWARE	OTHERS LEAD
SELF	SELF AWARE	SELF LEAD

SELF-AWARENESS

Our ability to practice a sober and accurate view of ourselves, for better and worse.

	AWARE	LEAD
OTHERS		
SELF	HONESTY HUMILITY SELF-LOVE	

Honesty

As we grow older, there is an assumption that we'll be more honest. However, as experience often reveals, being honest with ourselves and others is an ongoing challenge. Why? First, we cannot practice honesty in isolation. We all have blind spots and need feedback from our environment to help us see what we cannot see. We see ourselves more clearly reflected in the way we impact others. Developing a more honest and accurate view of ourselves is paramount to growth because you can't change what you can't see.

You can't change
what you can't see.

Second, we will often discover things about ourselves we don't like, that stir feelings of shame, guilt, or regret. We're tempted to hide our worst bits for fear of judgment and rejection. We fear our failures and inadequacies will disqualify us from better things, so we cover them up or ignore them. Let me say this: I've never seen anyone disqualified from better things because they owned their shortcomings. It's just the opposite.

Honesty is asking ourselves the tough questions. *Why did I lose my temper? Why am I shrinking back in this meeting? Why did I make those injurious comments? Why am I not doing what I said I would do?* We may not always get to the bottom of what's going on in our minds, but by asking ourselves these hard questions, it will go a long way toward greater self-awareness.

Let me illustrate this with a story. Take John, a mid-level manager who was always passed over for promotions. Frustrated, he blamed his colleagues and even his boss for not recognizing his hard work. One day, after another missed opportunity, he decided to seek feedback. He learned that his team found him unapproachable and resistant to new ideas. This was a hard pill to swallow, but by being honest with himself and acknowledging these blind spots, John began to work on his communication skills and openness. Over time, not only did his relationships improve, but he also finally earned that promotion.

Let's also remember that honesty about our strengths and successes is equally important, because it provides a balanced and accurate view of ourselves. Honesty requires we celebrate both the gold and the dirt of who we are. Recognizing what we do well builds confidence, motivates continued growth, and sets a positive example for others. When we celebrate our wins and own our strengths, we create a foundation of authenticity and resilience, which helps us navigate failures with a constructive mindset. This honesty allows us to fully appreciate our journey, leverage our unique capabilities, and learn from every experience—good or bad.

Humility

If honesty is seeing ourselves soberly and accurately, then humility is about accepting what we find. We can only be who we are today, not who we or others wish we were. You're not the same person you were last year, nor are you the same person you'll be a year from now. We are constantly evolving, but our inability to embrace the best and worst of who we are today causes us to try and be something we're not.

Humility embraces both the gold and the dirt we discover within ourselves, freeing us to bring our full selves to every situation. We get to play our cards and let the chips fall where they may. Sometimes we'll have a winning hand and sometimes we won't. But pretending to be something we're not is always a losing hand.

Self-Love

Self-love is the permission we must give ourselves to become a better version of ourselves. Too easily, we get stuck in a shame cycle regarding mistakes, failures, or deficiencies. The way we move forward is to practice self-love in two ways. First, practice

> Remember your superpower— **you get to choose.**

forgiveness toward yourself and others. We don't need years of therapy to practice forgiveness; it's a choice we make. A mentor once told me, "Forgiveness is free, but trust is earned." Forgiving ourselves and others for past injuries or errors is simply canceling the debt we hold onto. We think unforgiveness gives us power, but the opposite is actually true. I heard someone say, "Holding onto unforgiveness is like drinking poison hoping the other person dies." Remember your superpower—you get to choose.

Second, with the freedom that comes with forgiveness, commit yourself to practicing the best version of yourself. It's amazing when I ask clients, "What does the best version of you look like in this situation?" They almost always say something inspiring and helpful. We must forge ahead, giving ourselves permission for personal transformation and growth.

Lisa (a former client) was haunted by a mistake she made in a big project that cost her company a client. She couldn't forgive herself and was stuck in a cycle of self-blame, which caused her to shrink back during important meetings. It wasn't until she chose to forgive herself and learn from the experience that she could move forward. She committed to being the best version of herself and eventually led her team to secure even bigger clients.

SELF-LEADERSHIP

Our ability to operate with self-control, especially under pressure.

	AWARE	LEAD
OTHERS		
SELF	HONESTY HUMILITY SELF-LOVE	COMPOSURE FLEXIBILITY LEARNING

Composure

We all lose our shit on occasion. Remember, to be human is to get hijacked from time to time. The practice of composure is not a fake-it-till-you-make-it response. Instead, it is rooted in the belief that we are 100 percent responsible for our actions or reactions. Again, we cannot blame others for our attitudes and behaviors.

I'll illustrate the practice of composure with what we call the Swan Effect. On the surface, a swan glides effortlessly across the water, while underneath their legs may be working much harder to maintain or change movement. When triggered and on the brink of a hijacking, we get to choose our response. We can choose patience, silence, a smile, or clarifying questions. We also get to choose our body language to ensure we are communicating composure.

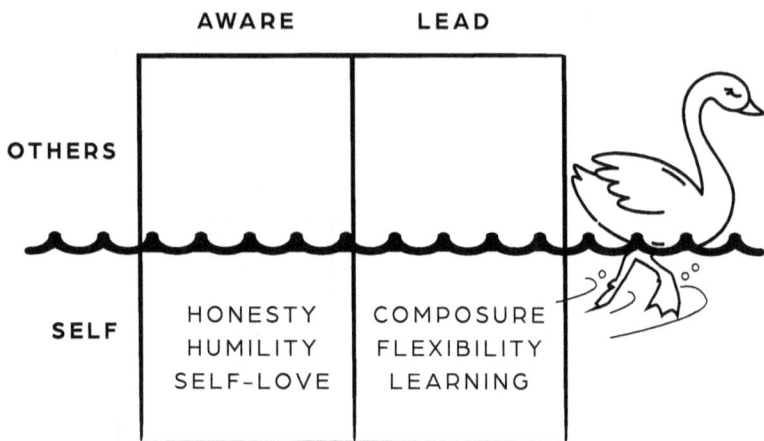

	AWARE	LEAD
OTHERS		
SELF	HONESTY HUMILITY SELF-LOVE	COMPOSURE FLEXIBILITY LEARNING

Composure is the practice of self-control. No matter how far down the hijacked pathway we find ourselves, once we realize we've lost our cool, we can practice honesty, humility, and self-love on our way back to composure.

Mark is a partner at a prestigious law firm who was known for his temper. In meetings, he often exploded when things didn't go as planned. One day, after a particularly harsh outburst, he noticed the discomfort and fear in his team's faces. After processing this incident with me, he realized the negative impact on his partners and committed himself to practicing greater composure. We set a strategy and plan to help him recognize when his emotions flare and how to recover his mental and emotional sobriety. The next time a project derailed, he took a deep breath, paused, and owned his triggered emotions before addressing the issue calmly. His team was shocked by his honesty and composure but thanked him for his gracious response. Their trust in him grew immensely that day.

Flexibility

This is our ability to bend without breaking. This reminds me of a story I once read about Jerry Rice's lengthy career in the NFL. He attributed his ongoing health and strength to a disciplined stretching routine. His flexibility allowed him to bend without breaking when tackled by men twice his size.

Practicing flexibility is recognizing that we all have expectations of how things in life will unfold. When expectations aren't met, many people break and either seek to bend the world to their expectations or withdraw from it. It's great to have expectations, but not to be ruled by them. The illustration below reminds us that our expectations, when held too tightly, become a bullseye. It's great when life hits the bullseye, but it rarely does. The target is much bigger than the bullseye. Flexibility is the practice of healthy compromise and adaptation, which still allows us to hit a target. And in working with others, an appropriate target usually affords more win-win solutions.

RIGID
EXPECTATIONS

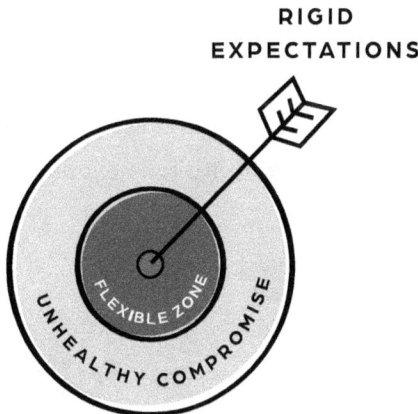

FLEXIBLE ZONE

UNHEALTHY COMPROMISE

Sarah, a project manager for a medical supply company, developed a detailed plan for a new product launch. When unexpected delays threatened the timeline, instead of rigidly sticking to the original plan, she adapted. She collaborated with her team to find alternative solutions, adjusting the schedule and reallocating resources. Her flexibility allowed the team to still meet the core objectives, even if the path was different than initially planned.

Learning

This is the pinnacle expression of self-leadership. I'm not talking about knowledge acquisition here, but the wisdom that comes from learning from our life experiences. Without the practice of the earlier EQ skills, we cannot grow in our wisdom. Wisdom is born out of intentional personal reflection on our experiences, asking what happened, why it happened that way, and what we can learn. Wisdom requires the discipline of both self-awareness and self-leadership.

A commitment to a growth mindset is a posture that leads to increased maturity and gravitas within our relationships. It allows others to trust us even when we fail. It's important to remind ourselves that the only true failure is failing to learn from our failures. We'll dig deeper into this skill with the next tool!

The only true failure is **failing to learn from our failures.**

OTHERS-AWARENESS

Our ability to see others soberly and accurately, to prioritize human connection.

	AWARE	LEAD
OTHERS	EMPATHY LISTENING BELIEF	
SELF	HONESTY HUMILITY SELF-LOVE	COMPOSURE FLEXIBILITY LEARNING

Empathy

Empathy is our ability to see and appreciate life from someone else's perspective, especially when they are different from you. It does not mean we have to agree with them, but it does mean we make an intentional effort to understand what another person is experiencing from within their frame of reference. If we're not careful, we'll find ourselves operating from assumptions that the world is the way we think it is. Worse yet, in our conviction, we close ourselves off from other perspectives, thereby robbing ourselves of opportunities to increase our understanding and intelligence.

In the same way that we can't change what we can't see, it's also true that we can't serve what we can't see. Great leadership is always in service of others. So how can we serve others if we don't understand or appreciate them? Too often, we engage others ignorantly or naively, consumed with our own views, when a little bit of curiosity would have revealed the insights we need to handle others well.

Great leadership is always in service of others.

Virtually every great ambition in life requires that we partner with others. Empathy is the practice of prioritizing those relational connections, not just the desired outcomes. Beware lest you find yourself sacrificing people on the altar of productivity and profits. It's never worth it.

Tom, a manager within a healthcare office, often pushed for results while overlooking his team's feelings. When turnover became an issue, he was forced to acknowledge something was wrong. After a conversation with one of our coaches, he realized his lack of empathy was costing everyone around him. He started to listen to his team's concerns and made significant attempts at understanding their challenges. This shift not only improved morale but also boosted productivity, as team members felt heard and valued.

In working with others, we cannot afford to overlook the fundamental need all people have to feel seen, heard and valued. We cannot give trust or our best work when this need is unmet. Empathy is the practice of making others feel seen, heard and valued for what they bring, regardless of whether we see eye-to-eye.

Listening

This is another discipline of curiosity, where we seek to understand where people are coming from in conversations. We must learn to pay attention not only to the words coming from their mouths, but also to their body language and their background. Rarely do people say what they mean the first time around, and so much gets lost in translation, which usually leads to misunderstanding, misinterpretation, unnecessary conflict, and disconnection in relationships.

We must practice active and reflective listening. Active listening is showing up to a conversation with the intention of listening, learning, and understanding. It's showing up with your whole self, not just your ears. Reflective listening is the discipline of asking clarifying questions, reflecting what you're hearing, and ensuring the person talking feels heard and understood before we respond. It's impossible to listen well when your mind is scrambling with a response before the other party has finished speaking!

Emily, a department head at a growing software company, often found her team silent and unengaged during meetings. After interviewing her team, we discovered they felt overpowered by Emily's communication style. She realized she wasn't truly listening to her team—she was too busy planning her responses and often shut down their ideas before they felt heard. She decided to practice active listening. In the next meeting, she focused entirely on what was being said, asked clarifying questions, and her team noticed. Communication improved, and so did the team's effectiveness.

Belief

We cannot lead others well if we do not believe they can become a better version of themselves. In the previous chapter on the RMS, we acknowledged that we're all going to fall short in our performance from time to time. In the same way that self-awareness gives us permission to fail forward, we must be willing to do the same for others. Part of great leadership is seeing the potential in others, despite their shortcomings, and investing in their growth and development. This requires we believe in a better version of others.

> **Great leadership is seeing the potential in others,** despite their shortcomings, and investing in their growth.

Believing in others is acknowledging their gold and dirt, while giving them ample opportunity to dig through their dirt for more gold. If we find that our perception of someone has gone negative, we must first check ourselves to ensure we are not operating from a negativity bias. Then, we can go back to the practices of empathy and listening to discover where our team members need our help.

Again, believing in others doesn't mean we agree with them or tolerate them falling below our RMS. Believing in others is how we empower them to become a better version of themselves.

OTHERS-LEADERSHIP

Our ability and willingness to leverage the resources at our disposal for the best interest of all parties involved.

	AWARE	LEAD
OTHERS	EMPATHY LISTENING BELIEF	COMMUNICATION CONFLICT DEVELOPMENT
SELF	HONESTY HUMILITY SELF-LOVE	COMPOSURE FLEXIBILITY LEARNING

Communication

We all communicate, but we don't all communicate effectively. This skill is made even more difficult because we think that by speaking the same language, effective communication should follow. However, anyone who's been married knows that just because we speak the same language, it doesn't mean we'll communicate successfully.

Great communication requires three essential elements:

1. Shared Language: This is more than just the same dialect. In the same way that every industry has its own distinctive lingo, which makes communication easier, every team and organization requires a shared leadership lingo. What you

will discover throughout this book is a simple, shared leadership language that helps everyone get on the same page when processing, making decisions, engaging conflict, and the like.

2. Shared Meaning: It's critical that we all mean the same thing by what we say. It is a frequent occurrence for me to mediate in meetings where we discover multiple parties had different understandings even though they were using the same language. For example, what time is actually meant by EOD (End of Day)? You'd be surprised how many conflicts have arisen because the parties involved understood this differently.

3. Shared Practices: I'm always nervous when someone tells me they love conflict. They may love it, but that usually means they're not very good at it. Conflict (as we'll soon discover) is a necessary part of working with others, but if everyone engages in conflict differently, then it will lead to disaster. We need shared practices for the key leadership responsibilities within our environment to give us the best chance of moving forward well.

Once, I worked with a team that was constantly missing deadlines. Upon investigation, it turned out that everyone had a different understanding of what "ASAP" meant. By establishing shared language and clear practices, the team improved their communication and met their targets consistently.

Conflict

Why does conflict feel like a four-letter word? Why do we dread conflict and avoid it like the plague? Simply, most of us have a terrible track record when it comes to the experience of conflict engagement. Our parents may have yelled, thrown things, cursed, or used physical intimidation when things got heated. We have likely experienced passive, aggressive, or passive-aggressive behaviors from friends or coworkers. Most of us have lost connection to friends or loved ones because a conflict was handled poorly.

We have to flip the script on conflict engagement by reframing it for what it is. Conflict is a gift. That's right, conflict simply reflects differing perspectives, convictions, or expectations among the various parties. Could you imagine if everyone in the world thought exactly as you? That would be a scary place. The real problem in conflict is that we feel threatened by a different perspective and give way to those harmful default attitudes and behaviors. When we're operating from self-protection, the worst version of ourselves jumps back into the driver's seat, and the only option now is a win-lose conclusion. When we choose to see conflict for what it is, we are free to practice composure, flexibility, learning, empathy, listening, and belief to find a win-win solution.

Conflict is a gift.

At a company I consulted for, two departments were at odds over resource allocation. Instead of avoiding the conflict, the leaders brought everyone together to openly discuss their needs and concerns. Through effective communication and mutual understanding, they found a solution that benefited both departments, turning a potential clash into a collaborative success.

It's helpful to remember that by practicing the skills of Other-Awareness (Empathy, Listening, Belief), we set ourselves up to engage in conflict with far greater results.

Development

This is the pinnacle expression of great leadership! In the same way that parents (in their best moments) want their kids to do better than they have, great leaders seek to leverage their strengths to help others elevate their character, competency, and capacity. In other words, a developmental mindset seeks to make our ceiling their floor.

There are three key reasons leaders don't operate with a developmental mindset:

1. They did not experience the benefits of developmental leaders in their journey and therefore don't have a reference point for it.

2. They believe intentionally developing others takes too much time and therefore outsource all development to HR or third parties.

3. They are insecure and fear developing leaders beneath them will threaten their own job security.

All human progress stems from people who go further than the generation before them.

All human progress stems from people who go further than the generation before them. Embracing a developmental mindset makes us an asset to our teams, our organizations, and society at large as we lift those around us to go as far as they can.

Steve is a senior engineer who took time to mentor junior staff despite his heavy workload. His efforts didn't go unnoticed—those he mentored became top performers, driving innovation within the company. Steve's willingness to develop others not only benefited the team but also enhanced his own reputation as a leader.

(For a deeper dive into this tool, please check out *Leadership Gravitas,* by Eric Pfeiffer, 2021.)

TAKEAWAYS

- Emotional intelligence is foundational to great leadership and starts with mastering oneself.

- The EQ Matrix provides a framework for understanding and improving our relationships with ourselves and others through awareness and leadership.

- As leaders, we can only give to others what we first cultivate within ourselves.

- Leaders define culture by the attitudes and behaviors they practice most.

REFLECTION QUESTIONS

- In which quadrant of the EQ Matrix do you feel strongest, and which one needs more attention?

- Can you recall a recent situation where practicing self-awareness or self-leadership could have led to a different outcome?

- How can you apply the concepts of empathy and listening to improve relationships in your personal or professional life?

- What steps can you take to develop others around you, and how might this impact your team or organization?

By delving beneath the surface and mastering the EQ Matrix, we unlock the true power of transformational leadership. It's a journey worth taking—for us and for those we lead.

06

KAIROS CIRCLE

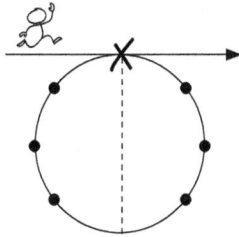

CHANGE EVERY CHALLENGE INTO LEARNING AND BREAKTHROUGH

The MPWR LOS must empower us to change when needed and hold the line when necessary. As we age, the temptation grows to embrace the false belief: *"Old dogs can't learn new tricks."* But change and transformation are wired into our DNA. When we stop changing, we stagnate, and so do our companies.

I often remind my clients, "Every experience in our life is an opportunity to learn, transform, and grow." This statement holds true for every situation we face, whether big or small, positive or negative. Each moment contains a wealth of insight, understanding, and wisdom waiting for us to excavate. The key is whether we choose to see challenging moments as threats or golden opportunities to gain wisdom.

Life is full of moments we often rush past or avoid altogether. Sometimes it's because we lack the courage to confront a challenge, or perhaps we're simply in a hurry. The tool we'll explore in this chapter, the Kairos Circle, is what I consider the most powerful leadership tool at our disposal. Why? Because it equips us for continual transformation and growth.

Kairos Moments: What They Are and Why They Matter

The Greeks had a fascinating view of time. The horizontal line in the diagram represents *Chronos*, or chronological time—linear time that ticks forward, marking the progression of days, months, and years. We experience this as the ordinary passage of time, the daily grind of life. But along this timeline, there's another kind of time the Greeks called *Kairos*. These are the moments when life shakes us up—mentally, emotionally, or physically. These disruptions can be big or small, positive or negative, but they all share one thing in common: every Kairos moment is an invitation to learn, grow, and transform.

In an earlier chapter, we discussed *triggers*—those moments that disrupt our equilibrium and stir up strong emotional reactions. Triggers are synonymous with Kairos moments. But here's where the shift happens: every Kairos moment is a portal. It's an opportunity to step through it into greater wisdom, self-awareness, and leadership growth.

Leaning into "Speed Bumps"

Unfortunately, most of us treat Kairos moments like inconvenient speed bumps. We rush over them, trying to avoid the discomfort, eager to move on to the next thing without bottoming out. But what if, instead of speeding past, we slowed down and leaned into these moments?

Let me share a story. I was working with an executive who had been struggling with his team. One afternoon, he called me, his voice full of excitement. "Eric, we had a major breakthrough this week—all because of the Kairos stuff you've been teaching us!" I could hear how energized he was, so I asked him to explain.

"One of our staff accidentally sent out highly confidential pricing information to all of our clients. It was a disaster. The entire executive team was hijacked—we were angry, blaming each other, and ready to find someone to fire. But then I remembered that this was a Kairos moment. I stopped the meeting and reminded the team: we could either see this as a catastrophe or an opportunity. The energy in the room shifted, and we all worked together to solve the issue. What we found were major gaps in our internal communication systems that needed fixing. This Kairos moment ended up transforming how we communicate as a team. The outcome was so much better than it would have been if we had just reacted in the usual way."

Processing a Kairos: Six Steps to Transformation

Every Kairos moment, no matter how difficult, offers a chance to practice personal responsibility. This leads to greater self-awareness and stronger leadership. When we process a Kairos effectively, we stop the downward spiral and choose an upward trajectory. Let's break down the six steps of processing a Kairos moment.

Every Kairos moment, no matter how difficult, **offers a chance to practice personal responsibility.**

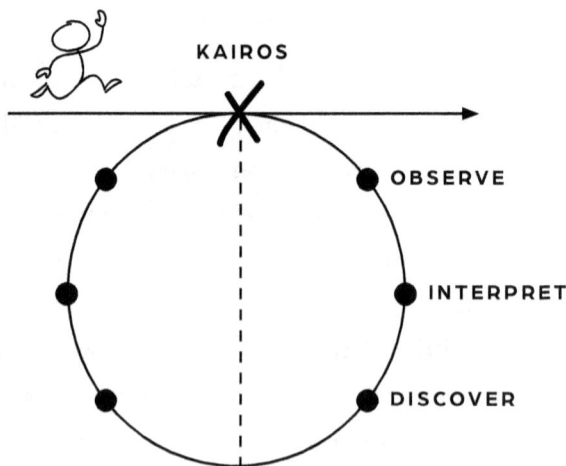

KAIROS

OBSERVE

INTERPRET

DISCOVER

Step 1: Observe (What Are the Facts and Feelings of This Kairos?)

We begin by simply observing what happened. This requires paying attention to two things: the facts and our feelings. Kairos moments usually stir strong emotions, which can easily distort our view of the facts. That's why it's important to seek input from others to ensure we're seeing things clearly.

> "If we don't own our feelings, **they will own us.**"

Acknowledging our emotions is critical. I often say, "If we don't own our feelings, they will own us." Recognizing that we've been emotionally disrupted allows us to regain clarity and prevent our emotions from clouding our judgment.

Step 2: Interpret (How Am I Making Sense of This Kairos?)

Next, we interpret the Kairos moment. Our experiences shape the lenses through which we see the world, and these lenses help us make sense of new experiences. But we must remember that our initial interpretation may not always be accurate.

To interpret a Kairos moment well, we need to:

1. Recognize that our first interpretation may be wrong.

2. Ask lots of clarifying questions: *Why did this happen? Why did I react this way? What emotions are driving my response?*

3. Invite others to give feedback on our interpretation to ensure it's grounded in reality.

Step 3: Discover (What Am I Learning, or What Are My Takeaways from This Kairos?)

Now we ask ourselves: *What am I learning from this?* Transformation begins when we uncover the insights hidden in our experiences. What are we learning about ourselves, others, and the situation? Taking the time to articulate these lessons not only sharpens our understanding but also solidifies the learning in our minds.

As we reflect, we may uncover limiting beliefs, distorted mindsets, or unhelpful internal narratives that cloud our ability to navigate situations effectively. This is the moment to name those distortions and intentionally choose beliefs or narratives that bring out a better version of ourselves. In my book, *Transform Your Trajectory*, I call this the *Great Exchange*—the process of trading old, unhelpful mindsets for new, empowering ones that propel us forward.

At the end of every coaching session, I ask participants to write down one key takeaway. This simple act of reflection—whether written or spoken aloud—cements the learning. Without this intentional practice, valuable lessons often slip through the cracks, leaving us unchanged by the very experiences meant to shape us.

Turning Learning into Action

The first half of the Kairos Circle helps us develop self-awareness. The second half is all about putting what we've learned into practice. Breakthroughs don't come from ideas alone—they come when we integrate those ideas into our daily lives.

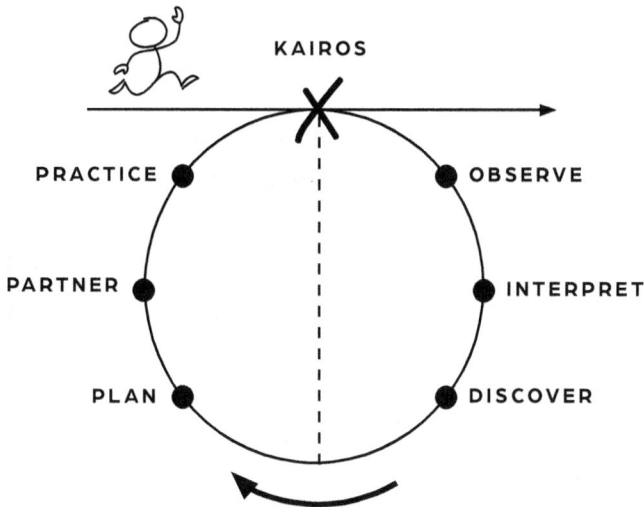

Step 4: Plan (What Is My Concrete and Calendarized Response to My Takeaway?)

Learning becomes wisdom when we act on it. Every Kairos moment should lead to a concrete, actionable plan. As Jim Rohn said, "Your life does not get better by chance; it gets better by change." But here's the catch: plans have to be specific and actionable. They don't start with, "I should..." or "I need to..." They start with, "I will..."

Good plans also need to be *calendarized*. If it's not on the calendar, it's unlikely to happen.

For example, "I will apologize to my wife for not returning her call by 6 p.m. tonight." Or "I will work out for 45 minutes on Monday, Wednesday, and Friday at 5:30 a.m."

Step 5: Partner (Who Will Provide Me the Support and Challenge I Need to Stick with My Plan?)

We're more likely to stick to our plans when we share them with someone else. This isn't about having someone police you—it's about finding a partner who can provide support and challenge. A good partner encourages you when motivation is low and holds you accountable when you're tempted to quit or make excuses.

Step 6: Practice (Have I Practiced My Plan and Is It Working?)

Remember, practice doesn't make perfect—it makes better. Some plans may require a one-time action, while others will need ongoing commitment. Either way, practice is essential. If you struggle to execute the plan, no worries—get back on track and keep practicing. Progress comes from consistent effort, not perfection.

Transforming Your Trajectory

When we process a Kairos moment, even imperfectly, we experience a shift in trajectory. We put the best version of ourselves in the driver's seat, elevating our leadership performance and unlocking new levels of growth. One of my coaches likes to say, "We can either spiral down or spiral up. Which do you prefer?"

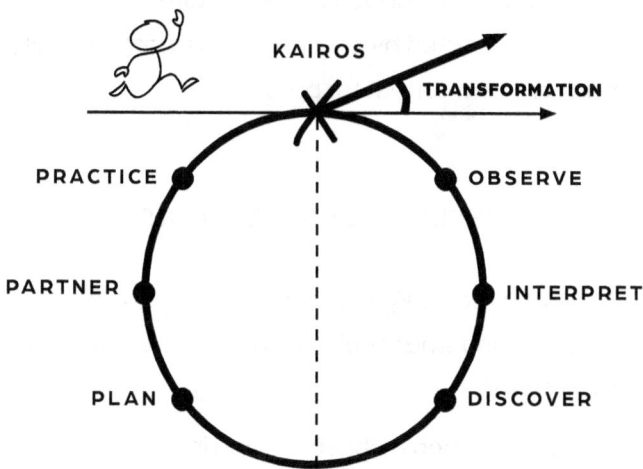

TAKEAWAYS

- Every Kairos moment is an opportunity to choose growth and transformation.

- Processing a Kairos helps increase self-awareness, personal responsibility, and leadership capability.

- Transformation happens when we turn learning into action, supported by concrete plans, accountability partners, and consistent practice.

REFLECTION QUESTIONS

- Think of a recent Kairos moment. How did you respond, and what could you have done differently to learn from it?

- How can you begin observing and interpreting your emotions in difficult situations rather than reacting impulsively?

- What specific action can you take today to turn a learning moment into a concrete, calendarized plan?

07

EMPOWER MATRIX

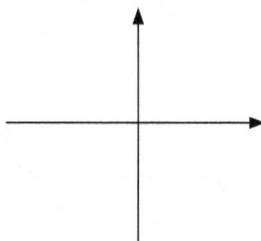

PARTNER WITH OTHERS TOWARD GROWTH AND TRANSFORMATION

Think back to the most empowering leader you've had in your life. Was it a parent, a teacher, a coach, a mentor, or even a boss? One of the core responsibilities of any leader is to bring out the best in the people they lead. The mindset of a great leader is simple: *If you win, we all win.* Leadership, at its heart, is a team sport.

I've always enjoyed watching documentaries about great sports teams—the pageantry, the blood, sweat, and tears that go into operating at peak performance over time. It's inspiring.

One thing is clear: behind every successful team, there's a great leader. Sometimes it's the coach, other times it's the team captain, but often, leadership is shared by multiple people who step up to create an empowering culture. This is the kind of culture where everyone levels up and thrives over the long haul.

And who doesn't want to be part of a winning team?

Yet, some teams excel while others, despite their talent, never reach their potential. The difference often comes down to culture. An empowering culture breathes life into every person, while a disempowering one can stifle even the most gifted individuals. But how do we create this empowering culture?

The Support and Challenge Matrix

Empowering leaders understand the importance of integrating a clear vision with the right amount of both support and challenge. This balance gives individuals and teams the best chance to succeed.

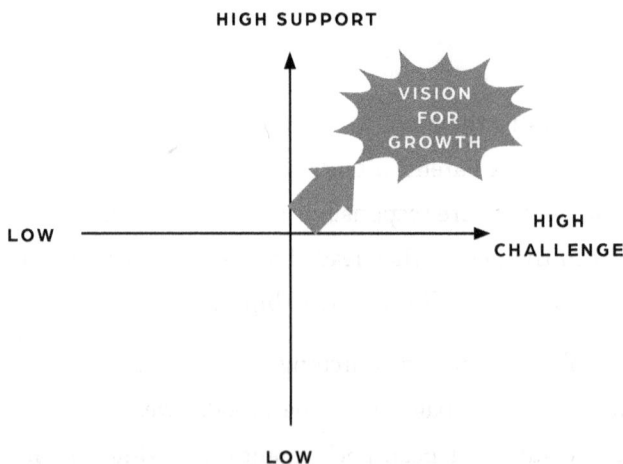

In the diagram above, the vertical axis represents the amount of support a leader provides, from low to high. The horizontal axis shows the level of challenge, from low to high. The sweet spot, where high support meets high challenge, is where an empowering culture is born.

Let's break it down.

What Do We Mean by Challenge?

We're talking about positive challenges here—the kind that sets clear expectations, boundaries, goals, and deadlines. It's about pushing people out of their comfort zones, holding them accountable, and embracing necessary conflict. Without a healthy amount of challenge, people stay in their familiar routines, miss opportunities for growth, and plateau. Every bit of personal and professional growth comes from being challenged—either by others or by ourselves.

What Do We Mean by Support?

Support comes through empathy, care, listening, encouragement, and believing in others when they struggle to believe in themselves. Support also includes fostering human connection, practicing vulnerability, and creating a sense of belonging. Without support, people become isolated, disconnected, and discouraged, leading to burnout.

High Support & High Challenge = Empowered Culture

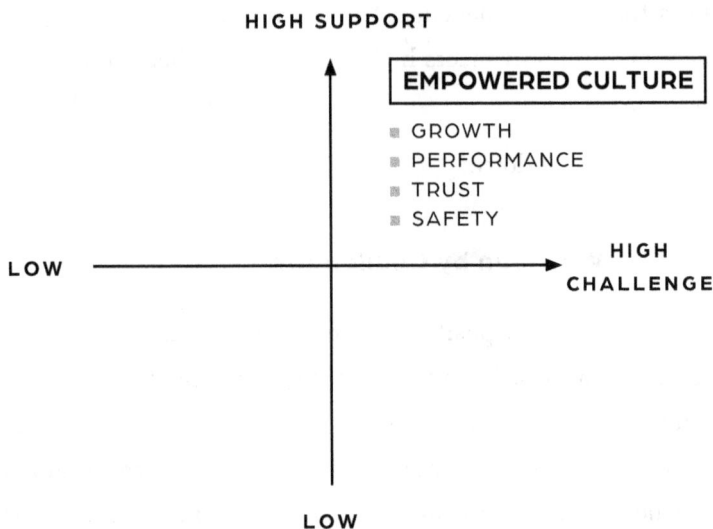

HIGH SUPPORT

EMPOWERED CULTURE

- GROWTH
- PERFORMANCE
- TRUST
- SAFETY

LOW →

HIGH
CHALLENGE

LOW

Most of us experience our greatest breakthroughs under leaders who offer clear vision and Radical Minimum Standards, along with a healthy balance of both support and challenge. In this empowered culture, people are given permission to fail forward, persevere through hardship, and practice vulnerability. These ingredients are essential for creating long-term growth.

Take Kate, a department head at a growing tech company. She believed in her team's potential but knew they needed to stretch themselves. Kate consistently provided clear direction and high standards while also creating an environment where team members felt safe to take risks and fail forward. When a major product deadline was looming, rather than micromanaging, she encouraged her team to experiment and solve problems creatively, offering guidance only when necessary. The result? The team not only hit their deadline but exceeded performance expectations because they were empowered to think and act like leaders themselves. The balance between challenge and support gave them the confidence to innovate.

Take a moment to reflect on these questions:

- Can you identify a leader in your life who empowered you with both support and challenge? What did that look like?

- Have you had a leader who provided only support or only challenge? How did that impact you?

- Do you feel more comfortable offering support or challenging others? (This may vary depending on the context.)

- Are you better at calibrating support or challenge with yourself?

The Other Quadrants: Culture Gone Wrong

Now let's explore what happens when support and challenge aren't balanced.

High Support & Low Challenge = Cozy Culture

When support is high but challenge is low, people get too comfortable. Without clear expectations or accountability, there's no incentive to push harder or go further. This "cozy culture" often results in people feeling coddled, complacent, and entitled. Why bother striving for more when no one expects you to? Words like *pampered* and *spoiled* often come up when describing this environment.

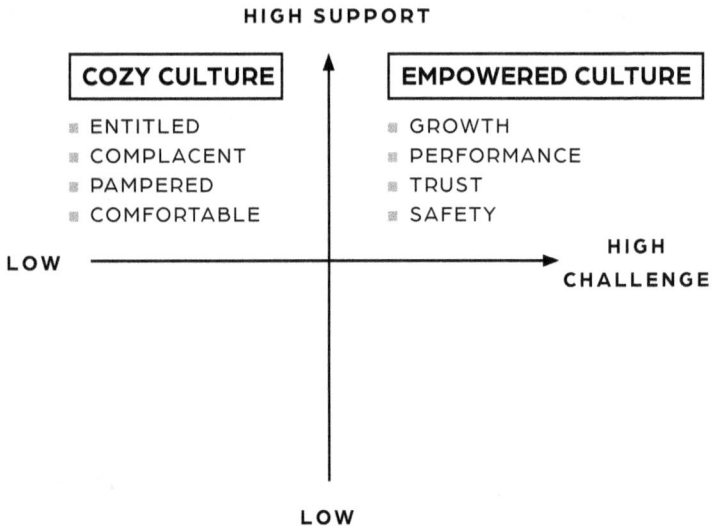

HIGH SUPPORT

COZY CULTURE	EMPOWERED CULTURE
▧ ENTITLED	▧ GROWTH
▧ COMPLACENT	▧ PERFORMANCE
▧ PAMPERED	▧ TRUST
▧ COMFORTABLE	▧ SAFETY

LOW ──────────────────────▶ HIGH CHALLENGE

LOW

The comfort of a cozy culture is deceptive. On the surface, everything seems pleasant—people get along well, there's little conflict, and everyone appears satisfied. But dig a little deeper, and you'll find that this sense of comfort has a cost: people become complacent. Without challenges to push them, individuals stop striving for more. The team may hit a plateau where innovation stalls and personal growth grinds to a halt.

Without challenges to push them, individuals stop striving for more.

John, a high-performing sales manager, experienced this first-hand. For years, he thrived in a supportive, laid-back environment where expectations were minimal. But after a while, he noticed his own enthusiasm waning. He wasn't being pushed to grow, and his performance, which once soared, started to stagnate. It wasn't until a new leader came in, raising the bar and holding John accountable, that he found drive and increased success again.

High Challenge & Low Support = Stressed Culture

HIGH SUPPORT

COZY CULTURE	EMPOWERED CULTURE
▣ ENTITLED	▣ GROWTH
▣ COMPLACENT	▣ PERFORMANCE
▣ PAMPERED	▣ TRUST
▣ COMFORTABLE	▣ SAFETY

LOW ⟶ HIGH CHALLENGE

STRESSED CULTURE

▣ FATIGUE
▣ EXHAUSTED
▣ BURNOUT
▣ TREADMILL OF APPROVAL

LOW

High challenge without adequate support creates a culture of discouragement. People might even push themselves hard, but without the encouragement and care they need, they eventually burn out. "No one appreciates the work I'm doing." "I feel like a cog in a machine." "I don't trust anyone here." These are the common complaints I hear from individuals stuck in this culture. It's a place where enthusiasm and engagement fade. Clients often describe this environment with words like *harsh, exhausting,* and *stressed.*

In a discouraged culture, leaders push hard for results but often forget the human element. Over time, this creates a pressure-cooker environment where employees feel undervalued and disconnected. Think of Sarah, a mid-level manager in a fast-paced corporate environment. Her boss demanded perfection and held the team to impossibly high standards. While the company was profitable, morale was rock-bottom. Sarah began dreading each day at work. The constant pressure, without any encouragement or support from leadership, drained her energy. She frequently heard her colleagues express feelings of isolation. "I feel like no one even notices the effort I put in," one coworker said. Eventually, several team members, including Sarah, burned out and either left the company or disengaged entirely. The high challenge with no support had created a toxic, unsustainable environment.

> In a discouraged culture, leaders push hard for results **but often forget the human element.**

Low Support & Low Challenge = Apathetic Culture

When there's neither support nor challenge, the result is an apathetic culture. This is a dead or dying environment where people may coexist, but there's no meaningful interaction or progress. With the rise of remote work, one of the biggest concerns I hear from leaders is how to prevent their teams from slipping into this quadrant due to limited in-person engagement. While it's possible to create structures that keep remote workers engaged, the risk of an apathetic culture is real.

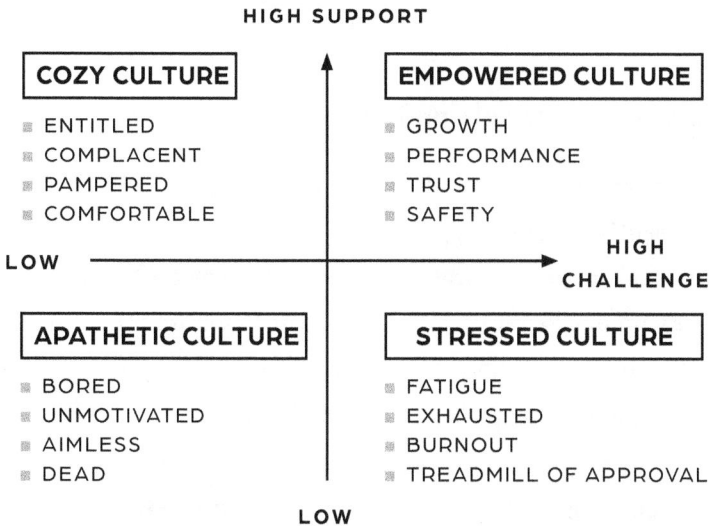

HIGH SUPPORT

COZY CULTURE	EMPOWERED CULTURE
▓ ENTITLED	▓ GROWTH
▓ COMPLACENT	▓ PERFORMANCE
▓ PAMPERED	▓ TRUST
▓ COMFORTABLE	▓ SAFETY

LOW ——————————————————————→ HIGH CHALLENGE

APATHETIC CULTURE	STRESSED CULTURE
▓ BORED	▓ FATIGUE
▓ UNMOTIVATED	▓ EXHAUSTED
▓ AIMLESS	▓ BURNOUT
▓ DEAD	▓ TREADMILL OF APPROVAL

LOW

An apathetic culture often sneaks in unnoticed. It's not always the result of active disengagement but can creep in slowly as a result of neglect. Leaders who don't challenge or support their teams inadvertently create an environment where people just go through the motions. Meetings become routine, projects are completed with minimal enthusiasm, and any sense of ambition or drive slowly dissipates.

Jessica, a project manager, noticed this happening with her team over time. After shifting to remote work, the team's once lively collaboration turned into brief, transactional interactions.

No one asked questions or offered ideas anymore. The team was meeting deadlines, but there was no energy, no passion. Eventually, Jessica realized they had slipped into an apathetic culture. The warning signs had been there: people stopped volunteering for extra responsibilities, innovation came to a standstill, and the usual camaraderie was missing.

Calibrating Support and Challenge

Because everyone responds differently to support and challenge, it's essential to adjust your approach based on the needs of the individual or group. Leadership is part science and part art— there's no one-size-fits-all solution. But the more intentional we are in calibrating support and challenge, the better the results we'll see. Remember, practice makes better!

Applications of the Support & Challenge Matrix

Let's explore two practical ways you can use this matrix.

1. The Empowerment Roadmap

Think of the matrix as a roadmap. You can plot yourself or others in any quadrant and ask: *What needs to change to move into the Empowered Quadrant?* For instance, if you realize your fitness journey has landed in the *Cozy* quadrant, you know you need more challenge. Maybe that means hiring a personal trainer or joining a class. Similarly, if a team member is stuck in the *Stressed* quadrant, spend some time exploring their struggles and offering the support they need to move forward.

HIGH SUPPORT

COZY   EMPOWERED

LOW   HIGH
                                         CHALLENGE

APATHETIC   STRESSED

LOW

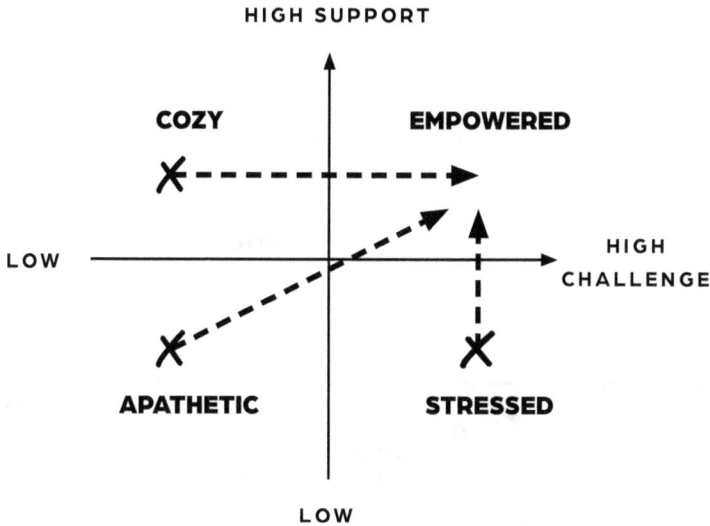

The Support & Challenge Matrix can also be a personal road-map. Let's say you've noticed that your professional development has hit a lull. By plotting yourself on the matrix, you might real-ize you've been stuck in the cozy quadrant, with lots of support but not enough challenge to push you forward. Maybe you've been avoiding taking on a new project or learning a new skill because no one is pushing you out of your comfort zone. The solution? Increase the challenge by setting yourself a stretch goal—like sign-ing up for a challenging course or taking on a new responsibility at work. On the flip side, if you're feeling overwhelmed and discon-nected from your team, it might be because you're experiencing too much challenge and not enough support. In that case, seeking mentorship or asking for help could provide the balance you need to shift into the Empowered Quadrant.

2. Creating a Growth Lane

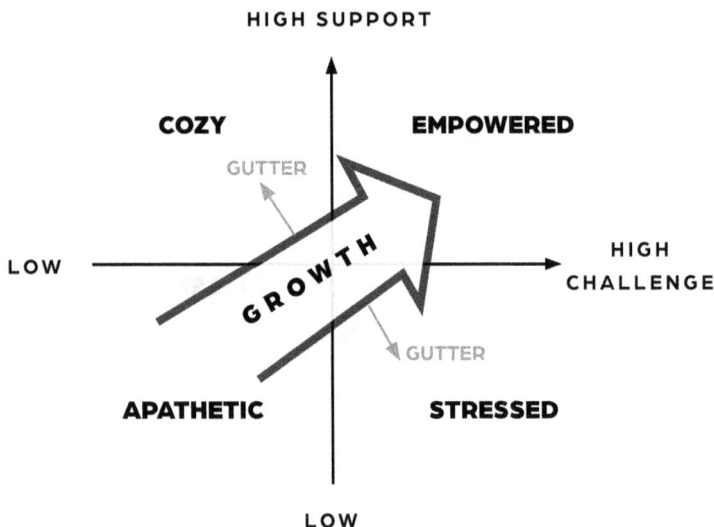

HIGH SUPPORT

COZY   EMPOWERED

GUTTER

LOW   HIGH
GROWTH   CHALLENGE

GUTTER

APATHETIC   STRESSED

LOW

To move or keep people in the Empowered Quadrant, we need to ensure a clarified vision, Radical Minimum Standards, goals, or objectives, then provide the right balance of support and challenge. This creates what I call the *growth lane*. It keeps individuals from falling into the "gutters" of the other quadrants and gives them the best chance to grow, perform, and thrive.

It's helpful to remember that without the intentionally applied energies of support and challenge, people and teams naturally stagnate and eventually find themselves in the Apathetic Quadrant. The Law of Entropy suggests that people will tend toward greater disorder and less efficiency, unless there is intentional energy invested to help them move toward greater order and efficiency.

Part of our responsibility as leaders is to identify what support and challenge is needed by individuals and teams to help them move in the right direction.

Without the intentionally applied energies of support and challenge, people and teams naturally stagnate and eventually find themselves in the Apathetic Quadrant.

TAKEAWAYS

- Empowering leadership balances high support with high challenge to create a culture of growth, performance, and trust.

- Too much support without challenge leads to complacency, while too much challenge without support leads to burnout.

- Calibrating support and challenge is both an art and a science, requiring intention and flexibility.

REFLECTION QUESTIONS

- Where in your life or work do you currently experience each of the four quadrants?

- Think about a time when you achieved something significant. What kind of support and challenge helped you reach that goal?

- How can you better calibrate support and challenge in your own leadership or personal development?

08

DEVELOPMENT SQUARE

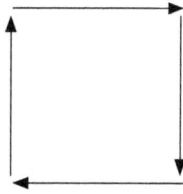

REPRODUCE LEADERS WHO
REPRODUCE LEADERS

From the moment we were conceived in our mother's womb, we have been on a continuous journey of growth and development. Growth is hardwired into our DNA. Biology plays a big part in the physiological development of our bodies, minds, and personalities. However, as we learned from caretakers, teachers, coaches, and others, much of our development is shaped by societal expectations—by the skills we need to learn to survive and advance in the world.

Some skills, like learning to walk, are necessary for survival. Others, like playing soccer or mastering culinary arts, reflect societal values and creativity. Whether it's brushing your teeth, riding a bike, mastering mathematics, or raising a family, everything we do represents a developmental journey. No one is born an expert at any of these things. In fact, no one is born an expert in anything. Every area of our life worth growing in requires a developmental process.

The Journey from Incompetence to Mastery

Let me ask you a question: How did you learn to brush your teeth? Or drive a car? Or do anything that you are really good at today? Most people stumble when answering. They might say, "I don't really remember. I just learned." That feeling of being able to do something automatically without thinking about it is what we call *Unconscious Competence*. We all have it in many areas of our lives, but we often don't understand the process that got us there.

Now, let me ask you another question: Can you think of something you started but then gave up on? Maybe you quit because of the setbacks and struggles that inevitably come with any developmental journey. You might have told yourself it wasn't worth it, or perhaps there was something better out there. Sometimes quitting is the right decision. But more often, it's the pursuit of success, growth, and mastery that dies in the graveyard of struggle—not because the pursuit was wrong, but because we didn't understand that the struggle itself was a sign we were on the right track.

We didn't understand that the struggle itself was **a sign we were on the right track.**

I believe the greatest barrier to our own development—and our ability to help develop others—is not understanding the development process. This leads us to give up on ourselves and others too soon. As leaders, the highest expression of our work is the ability and willingness to leverage all we have to help others climb higher. Long after we're gone, our legacy will be in the people we propelled further than ourselves.

Once we understand the four basic phases of the developmental journey, we will feel equipped to engage our own growth with greater confidence. We'll also be able to partner with others in their pursuit of becoming a better version of themselves.

So, let's dive into the Development Square, part of the MPWR LOS.

A Vision for Growth

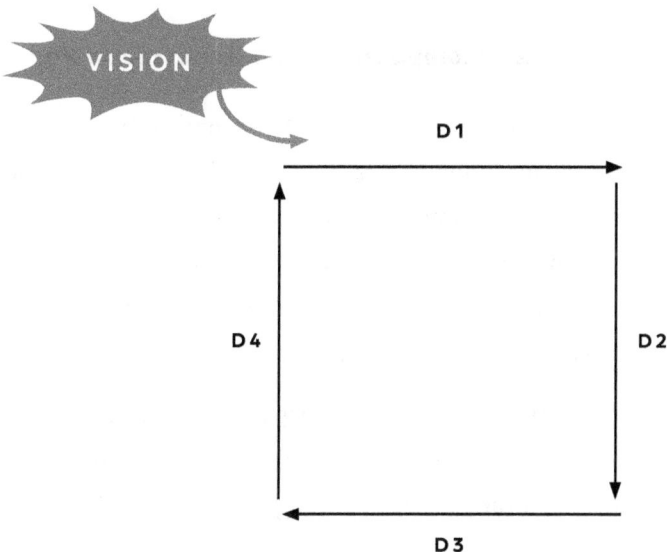

Our developmental journey usually begins with a vision for something better. Sometimes, this vision comes from within, like the time I saw my older brother riding a bike and decided I had to learn too. Other times, it's imposed upon us—like when your parents decided you were ready to do your own laundry, or your boss told you it was time for your first solo sales call. While it's more inspiring when the vision comes from within, thank goodness for those leaders who pushed us to grow, even when we protested. After all, that's how we became who we are today.

Reflect on an area of growth in your life that was driven by someone else pushing you. Are you grateful for their leadership? Do you think you would have achieved that success without them? Leadership isn't just about guiding others—it's about creating the conditions for others to thrive.

The Four Phases of Development

D1: Unconscious Incompetence (The Honeymoon Phase)

Phase 1 of the Development Square (D1) is marked by the experience of *Unconscious Incompetence*. This is the honeymoon phase—the beginning of a new adventure. We're excited, enthusiastic, and maybe a little naive. We don't know what we don't know. In this stage, we often dive headfirst into something new with a sense of naive confidence. Everything seems possible.

Remember the first time you tried something big—maybe learning a new job or starting a new hobby? You were full of energy, not yet aware of the challenges ahead. That's D1. This

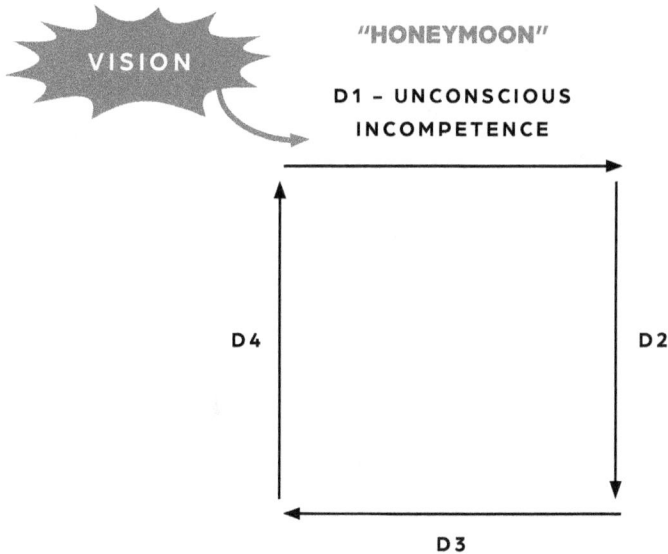

initial enthusiasm is critical because it provides the motivation to begin learning, even if that motivation is simply to keep your boss or coach happy.

But what happens when that enthusiasm hits a wall?

D2: Conscious Incompetence (The Pit)

When we take on any new venture, we inevitably run into a sobering reality: we don't actually know how to do the thing we're trying to learn. This might seem obvious, but as a leadership performance coach, I often work with highly successful individuals who are shocked by how difficult it can be to develop new abilities. Whether it's having tough conversations, launching a new division, navigating their relationship with the board, firing a longtime employee,

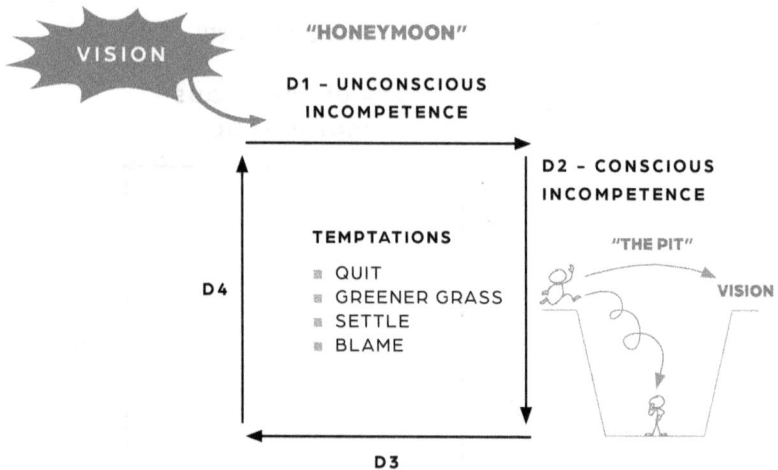

or carving out intentional time for their loved ones, the challenges feel daunting all over again.

D2 often feels like having the rug pulled out from under your feet—or worse, like stepping off a cliff and landing in a pit. This is where you come face-to-face with your own limitations, and the glaring exposure of incompetence is unsettling. Self-preservation mechanisms kick in, fear of humiliation rises, and you begin to question why you embarked on this journey in the first place. This is what we call **The Pit**—a phase that feels dark, lonely, and impossible to escape. No wonder it's marked by *No Confidence*.

> D2 often feels like **having the rug pulled out from under your feet**

In The Pit, we face powerful temptations: the urge to quit, to seek "greener grass," to settle for failure, or to blame others for the disorientation and discomfort we feel. Yet, it's here that the true fabric of our character is forged. We all know that our greatest internal growth happens in these dark, challenging moments, but when we're in The Pit, our rational mind works overtime to find the fastest way out. This is when doubling down on personal responsibility is critical. It requires embracing discomfort and leaning into the personal growth and maturity that can only be found in this space. Remember, we grow by stumbling and bumbling forward.

Remember, we grow by **stumbling and bumbling forward.**

Take a moment to reflect on a time when you were in The Pit (or perhaps you're in one now). What does The Pit feel like for you? Which temptations pull at you the hardest? Can you think of a time you persevered through a Pit, and what was the reward on the other side? The truth is, we've all endured countless Pits, emerged stronger, developed our character and skills, and lived to tell the stories.

Let me leave you with two encouraging thoughts:

1. D2, or The Pit, is an unavoidable part of any developmental journey—it cannot be skipped. While difficult, it's where you evolve into a better version of yourself.

2. You've already faced and overcome many Pits in your life, so take heart—you can handle many more.

D3: Conscious Competence (Growing Confidence)

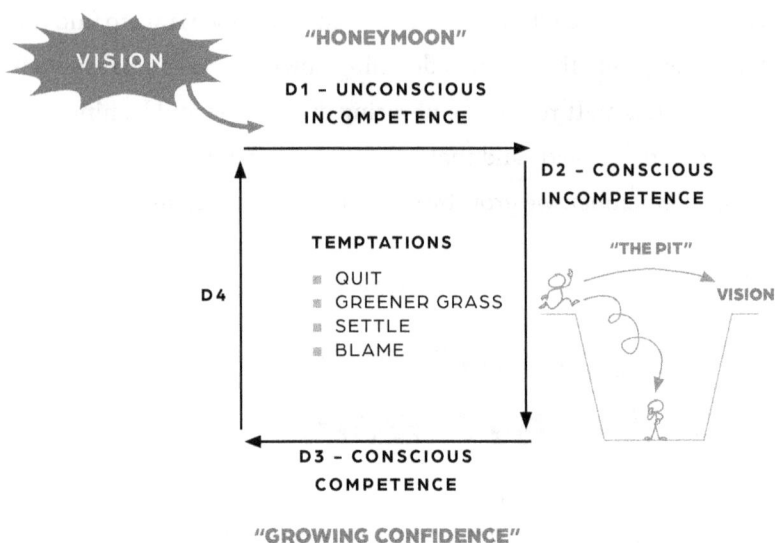

VISION

"HONEYMOON"

D1 – UNCONSCIOUS INCOMPETENCE

D2 – CONSCIOUS INCOMPETENCE

TEMPTATIONS

"THE PIT"

D4

- QUIT
- GREENER GRASS
- SETTLE
- BLAME

VISION

D3 – CONSCIOUS COMPETENCE

"GROWING CONFIDENCE"

If we push through D2, we reach D3, the experience of *Conscious Competence*. This is where things start to click. We're still putting in effort, but we're beginning to get the hang of it. Our confidence starts to return, but it's a tentative, growing confidence. It's like learning to ride a bike—wobbly at first, but then steadier with each try.

In this phase, practice is everything. We must test and reinforce our new skills repeatedly until they are solidified. Some people mistakenly believe they've mastered something as soon as they reach D3, but mastery comes from continual reinforcement. The more we practice, the more we own our new abilities.

Once in D3, the fog of The Pit lifts. Our progress is real, and we feel it. This is a critical time when leaders must continue providing guidance, ensuring that new skills take root.

D4: Unconscious Competence (Mastery)

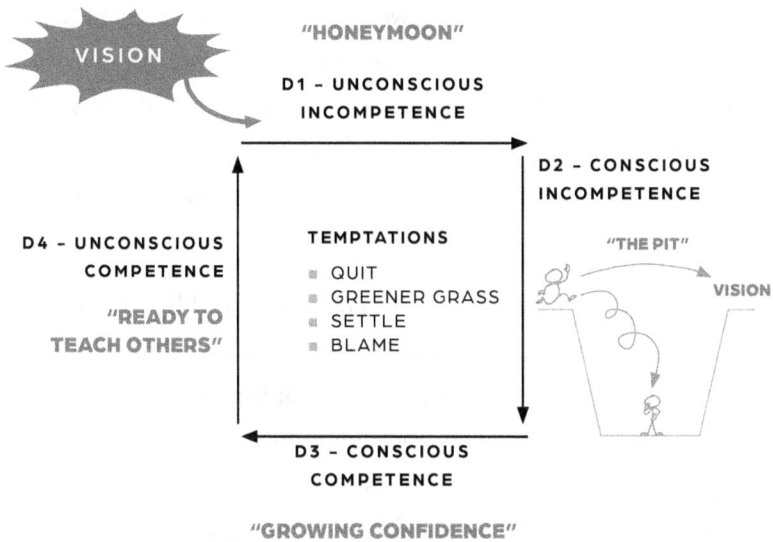

D4 is the stage of *Unconscious Competence*—the stage of mastery. We've practiced so much that the new skill becomes second nature. Think about how you drive to work without thinking about it or how you can navigate your phone without a second thought. In D4, the effort we once put in has been stored in our "permanent memory," freeing up mental energy for other tasks.

The reward of reaching D4 is increased mental margin. All the energy we once expended learning is now freed up. Our newly acquired skills have become a part of who we are. Just like when we learned to walk or type, these tasks are now hardwired into our subconscious, allowing us to use our mental bandwidth for new challenges.

Make Your Ceiling Their Floor

Joseph Campbell, in his classic work *A Hero with a Thousand Faces*, explains that we all play the hero in our own stories. We're driven to leave our old selves behind and set out on an adventure in search of something greater. Along the way, we face challenges, confront our inner demons, and forge new skills and character through trials.

As I've gotten older, my focus has shifted from identifying with the Hero to admiring the *Guide*—that wise, sage character who helps the Hero along their journey. The Guide provides encouragement, resources, perspective, and, sometimes, a well-timed kick in the pants. Think of Gandalf, Mr. Miyagi, or Obi-Wan Kenobi. The Guide exists to help the Hero reach their potential.

When we successfully navigate the Development Square ourselves, we are in the best position to help others on their own journeys. This is leadership development at its core. Our ceiling becomes their floor, and the cycle continues.

Great leaders know how to adapt their leadership style to the person's phase of development.

Let's take a look at the styles of leadership we can employ to best serve others on their developmental journeys.

Leadership in the Development Square

Helping others develop starts with understanding the stages of development: D1-D4. It's easy to mishandle people if we don't understand where they are. If we treat someone in D1 as if they're in D3, they'll be overwhelmed. If we treat someone in D3 as if they're in D1, they'll be frustrated and feel micromanaged. Great leaders know how to adapt their leadership style to the person's phase of development.

L1: I Do, You Watch (Directive Leadership)

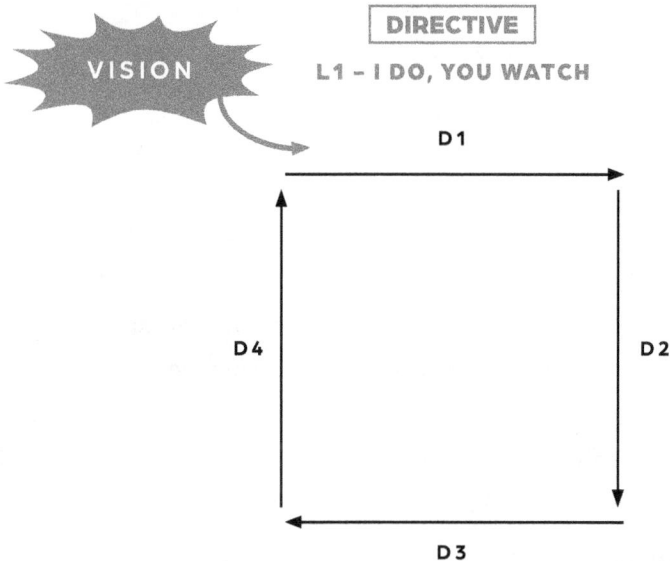

In D1, people need clear direction. They need to see how something is done before they can try it themselves. This is the *I Do, You Watch* phase. As leaders, we model the behavior we want to see.

We demonstrate, they observe. It's like teaching a child to tie their shoes—we first show them, step by step.

With small children, we instinctively understand the importance of modeling the behaviors we want them to imitate. Human beings are hardwired to learn through imitation. Every great athlete, artist, or investor first learned by copying the work of others. Once they mastered a skill set, they could innovate and create something new. The truth is this isn't just how we learn as children—it's how we learn throughout our entire lives. Whether we're imitating someone in person or through video, imitation is the gateway to innovation.

Imitation is the gateway to innovation.

L1 is a directive style of leadership where we determine how something should be done, model it ourselves, and then invite the other person to try it. Without a clear mental picture of how to do something, how can we expect anyone to know what's required? Yet how often are team members thrown into the deep end, expected to figure things out on their own, without ever being shown what success looks like? The answer is, too often.

When clients lament about a team member struggling to perform a task, I always ask, "Have you shown them how to do it?" More often than not, the answer is, "No." We've all heard the phrase, *Don't ask someone to do something you aren't willing to do yourself.* I'd add, *Don't ask someone to do something you haven't first modeled for them.*

L2: I Do, You Help (Coaching Leadership)

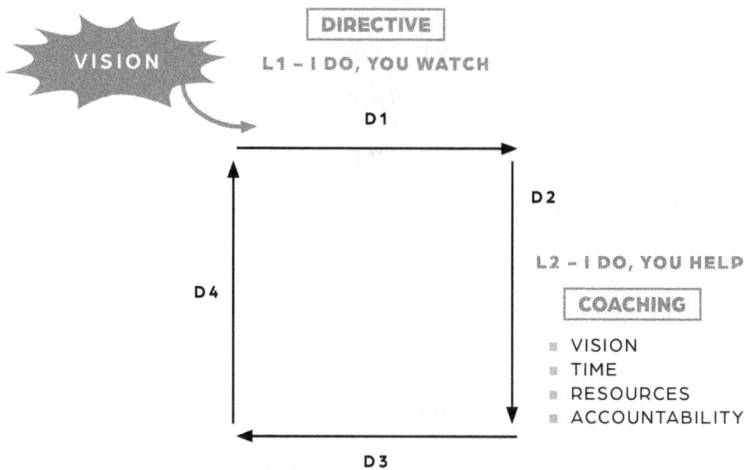

As we move into D2, we shift into the *I Do, You Help* phase. This is where coaching comes into play. People are going to stumble and struggle. It's our job to support them, offering vision, time, resources, and accountability as they work through The Pit.

If we want the people we're developing to move beyond D1, we must help them enter D2 by encouraging them to take a crack at the task they're trying to learn. But remember, as they step into D2, they'll face all the struggles we've already discussed. As leaders, we can't afford to be surprised or discouraged by this. Watching someone stumble and bumble their way through something can be exhausting. *"Ain't nobody got time for that!"* we might think. This frustration often leads us to take responsibility back, deciding it's easier if we just do it ourselves, or assuming our hero is destined to fail.

The truth is, L2 leadership demands more from us than any other phase because it's the most difficult for the person being developed. However, if we have any ambition to delegate responsibilities, multiply leaders within our organization, or help others truly flourish, we must persevere as L2 leaders.

Let's explore a few key strategies to guide someone effectively through their Pit.

Let's remember, as someone enters D2, they'll encounter four common temptations:

- **Quitting:** When the going gets tough, giving up can seem like the easiest escape.

- **Greener Grass:** They may believe the problem lies in their current role or environment and look for "better" opportunities elsewhere.

- **Settling for Failure:** Discouragement may lead them to stop trying altogether, accepting mediocrity.

- **Blaming Others:** To avoid owning their struggles, they may shift responsibility to external factors.

Leadership Handles for D2

This is where we, as leaders, must leverage support and challenge. By providing the right guardrails, we can help our hero avoid the gutters of complacency or burnout. Here's how:

1. Vision

When someone is tempted to quit, it's often because they've lost sight of what they're fighting for. Vision serves as a reminder of the reward waiting on the other side of the pain of growth. Without a clear picture of the goal, their energy and motivation will fade. As leaders, it's our job to regularly remind them why they're persevering. Sometimes this reminder feels like support; other times, it feels like a challenge. Either way, reconnecting them to the vision is essential for reinvigorating their commitment.

> **Reconnecting them to the vision is essential** for reinvigorating their commitment.

2. Time

The Pit can feel isolating, like no one truly understands what they're going through. This phase requires us to give extra time—checking in more often, offering additional assistance, or simply being available to listen. Sometimes, it means revisiting the task and showing them again what success looks like. I didn't particularly enjoy the seemingly endless process of potty-training my kids, but my motivation was simple: I didn't want to be wiping their rear-ends at sixteen! Patience and persistence are nonnegotiable in this phase. While we shouldn't smother or micromanage, the time we invest here is often seen as invaluable support.

3. Resources

Growth stalls when someone lacks the tools they need to succeed. Be attentive to ensure they have the right resources, whether that's additional training, access to a specialist, the right technology, or even a quieter workspace. Resources can make the difference between frustration and forward progress.

4. Accountability

It's tempting to ease up on accountability when someone is already struggling. We might think, *A little more pressure will break them.* But letting them off the hook entirely can be just as harmful. Growth requires steady expectations, even in the midst of struggle. While we may occasionally lighten the load, we can't afford to throw a pity party for someone in The Pit. Accountability provides the challenge they need to stay engaged and focused on the necessary steps for growth.

Growth requires steady expectations, even in the midst of struggle.

We cannot guarantee that someone will persevere through D2. However, by neglecting these four leadership skills—vision, time, resources, and accountability—we significantly reduce their chances of success. Perseverance isn't just a personal trait; it's something we can help nurture through intentional leadership engagement.

L3: You Do, I Help (Supportive Leadership)

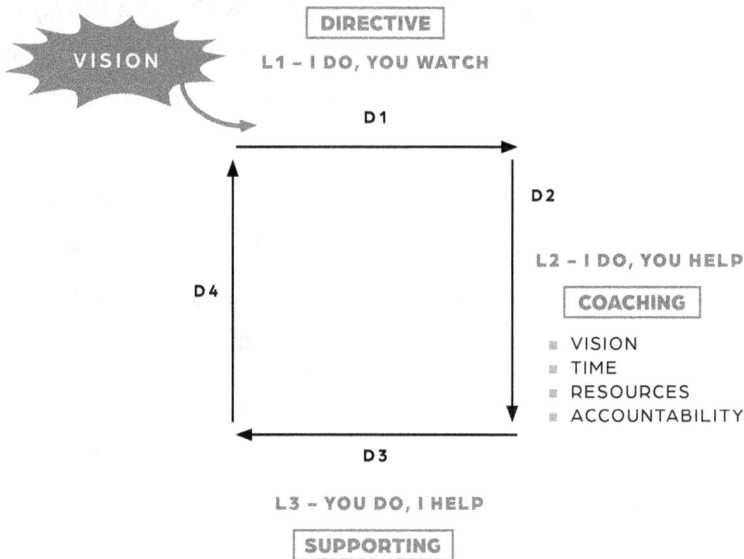

You'll notice your hero entering D3 when their attitude shifts to reflect growing confidence. They'll begin to take more initiative with their new responsibility—and we need to let them! This is the phase where we take our hands off the bike seat and allow them to fly. Of course, we remain close to offer support when needed, but the key transition in D3/L3 is a shift in who bears the primary responsibility. It's no longer ours—it's theirs.

Our role during this phase is to encourage them, remind them of what they've learned when necessary, and resist the temptation to take back control. They won't perform perfectly, and they might not do things exactly the way we did, but that's okay. This phase is critical for building the confidence they need to eventually do it better than we ever did.

That said, don't let their emerging confidence fool you. They'll still need to prove they can perform this new skill in a variety of contexts before you can completely shift your attention elsewhere. Mastery takes time, and part of our job is to provide the right balance of challenge and support to help them reach it.

Let me share this: there's no greater joy than watching one of my coaches not only do something I taught them, but watching them do it qualitatively better than I ever could. What's even more rewarding? Seeing them excel without needing my presence at all. That's when you know you've truly multiplied your leadership.

L4: You Do, I Watch (Delegating Leadership)

In D4, the person has mastered the skill. Now it's *You Do, I Watch*. We delegate fully and trust that they can handle the task without us. In fact, at this stage, they should be capable of training others.

> When we take development seriously, we ensure that **everyone is running on the same LOS.**

This is how we multiply leaders within our organizations. It's how we create sustainable cultures where everyone operates from the same playbook. When we take development seriously, we ensure that everyone is running on the same LOS.

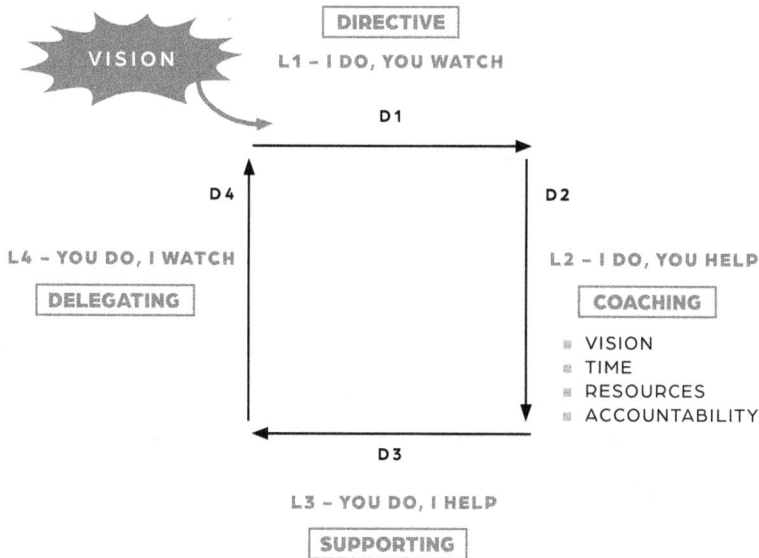

VISION

DIRECTIVE
L1 - I DO, YOU WATCH

D1

D4

D2

L4 - YOU DO, I WATCH

DELEGATING

L2 - I DO, YOU HELP

COACHING

- VISION
- TIME
- RESOURCES
- ACCOUNTABILITY

D3

L3 - YOU DO, I HELP

SUPPORTING

Years ago, I realized my personal capacity was finite. I could only work with so many clients, create so much content, and build certain business systems on my own. To extend my influence and impact, I needed to multiply my energy, my DNA, my skill set, and my mission. The Development & Leadership Square has become my primary framework for achieving this. Through it, I've multiplied myself in my children, in leaders and coaches trained in the LOS, and in organizations that continue to run the MPWR LOS. In this way, my legacy will live on long after I'm gone.

Tall Buildings Need Deep Foundations

As I write this, both of my children are in college and still largely financially dependent. In some areas, they've reached D4, but in others, they've just embarked on new areas of growth—entering new squares. With each new square they step into, they build upon the character and skills developed in previous journeys. Every trip around the square adds another layer to the foundation they'll rely on for the rest of their lives.

I hope this encourages you to reflect on the incredible foundation you've already built. Whether you realize it or not, you've completed hundreds of journeys around the square, shaping the person and leader you are today. The best part? There's always room for growth. The best leaders are growing leaders. As this tool illustrates, each layer you've built becomes a foundation for the next, not just for you, but for those you lead. You are always the hero of your own story, and at the same time, you serve others by making your ceiling their floor. The question is: How high do you want to go?

You are always the hero of your own story, and at the same time, you serve others by making your ceiling their floor.

TAKEAWAYS

- Growth is a journey that requires moving through stages of incompetence before reaching mastery.

- The Pit is a necessary part of development. It's where skills and character are forged.

- Great leaders know how to adjust their leadership style based on where the person is in their developmental journey.

REFLECTION QUESTIONS

- Where in your life are you currently in The Pit? How can you push through?

- Think of a time when someone helped you through a D2 phase. What made their leadership effective?

- How can you better calibrate your leadership style to the development phases of your team members?

09

LEADERSHIP PIPELINE

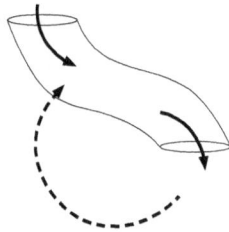

CREATE A CULTURE TO OPTIMIZE PERFORMANCE AND REDUCE TURNOVER

The Problem with Most Workplaces

Most organizations I've worked with have a clear hiring process, a somewhat defined training process, and almost no structured development pipeline. Companies are so intensely focused on delivering products or services that they neglect one of their most valuable assets—their people. When development is left to chance, employees quickly start to feel like cogs in the machine.

At first, they might be attracted to your company by a paycheck, benefits, or job security. But as time goes on, they'll start looking for something deeper: purpose, fulfillment, and the opportunity to grow. What's the cost of not providing that? Job hopping, disengagement, and ultimately a revolving door of talent leaving your organization.

The good news? You don't have to choose between a thriving business and an empowered workforce.

The solution lies in creating a Leadership Pipeline—a structured pathway that ensures everyone in your organization has the opportunity to develop and unlock more of their leadership potential. The good news? You don't have to choose between a thriving business and an empowered workforce. When you invest in your people, you're building a stronger engine for your organization's success.

The Leadership Pipeline

A pipeline is a direct channel that moves resources—whether liquids, gases, or in this case, talent—along a structured path. The Leadership Pipeline provides a clear process for identifying, developing, and promoting talent within your organization. It ensures that no one is left stagnant, and that the next generation of leaders is always being cultivated.

In this chapter, we'll walk through the four key stages of the Leadership Pipeline: Recruit, Train, Deploy, and Review. These stages will help your organization develop talent consistently and effectively, creating a thriving culture where both people and profits can grow.

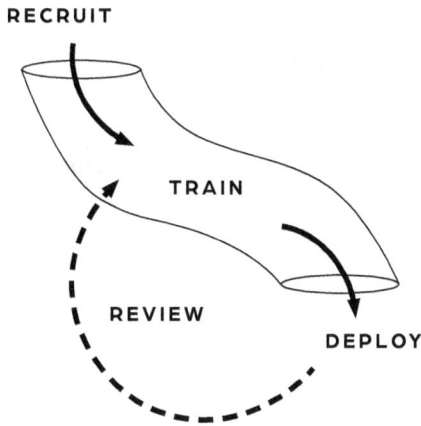

Recruit: Getting the Right People on the Bus

You get what you filter for. If you prioritize intelligence, you'll get intelligence. If your filter is simply a warm body to fill a position, that's exactly what you'll get. Recruiting is more than just filling vacancies—it's about bringing in the right people who will thrive within your organization's culture and grow into leadership roles.

Here are four key filters to consider during the recruitment process:

- Character: We often hire for competence and fire for character. While it's tricky to filter for character, it's essential. Check references thoroughly, ask character-based questions, and pay attention to how candidates treat everyone they interact with—from the receptionist to the CEO.

- Capacity: Does the candidate have the mental, emotional, and physical bandwidth to take on the role? If they're already maxed out in life, they may struggle to handle the pressures of the position. Look for signs that someone might be overwhelmed before they even step into the job.

- Chemistry: No matter how skilled someone is, if they don't mesh with the team, it won't work. Chemistry is about how well people can work together under pressure. Do they practice curiosity, self-awareness, and empathy? Do they handle conflict constructively?

- Competence: Finally, the baseline requirement for any role is the ability to perform the tasks required. Ensure they have the skills and know-how to hit the ground running— or at least the potential to learn quickly.

Train: Building Skills and Culture

Hiring great people is just the first step. Next, you have to train them—not just in the technical skills they need for their roles, but also in the culture you want to cultivate.

- Job-Related Training: This is the nuts and bolts of the job—the specific skills, systems, and processes required to perform their role effectively. But don't stop there. Crosstrain your employees to ensure they have a broad understanding of the company and can step into other roles when needed. This adds flexibility and resilience to your team.

- Culture Training: Culture is "how we do things around here." If you don't explicitly train your people in the culture, they'll default to their own preferences. This often leads to power struggles and dysfunction. Use the MPWR

LOS to instill a shared leadership language and set of practices, ensuring that everyone is on the same page when it comes to decision-making, communication, and conflict resolution.

If you don't explicitly train your people in the culture, they'll default to their own preferences.

Deploy: Getting the Right People in the Right Seats

Hiring and training people is great, but how intentional are you about deploying them? Are you putting people in the right roles that maximize their potential? Here are three key factors to consider when deploying your team:

- Clarity: Does your team know exactly what's expected of them? Too often, we assume people understand their responsibilities, only to discover later that they didn't. Clear goals, objectives, and measures are essential for success.

- Growth: Are you deploying your team members into roles that allow them to grow? Stagnation kills potential. Make sure people are given opportunities to step into new challenges and developmental squares, either within their current role or a new one.

- Fit: Don't just throw people into roles without considering whether it's the right fit for their skills and aspirations. Alignment between personal and professional goals is key to long-term success.

Review: Short Feedback Loops for Continuous Improvement

If your organization still relies solely on annual reviews for feedback, you're wasting your time. Annual reviews offer a low return on investment and fail to provide timely, actionable insights. Instead, implement short feedback loops to create an environment of continuous learning and improvement.

Here's how to approach feedback more effectively:

- Purpose of Feedback: Every feedback session is a Kairos moment—an opportunity to reflect on what's working and what's not. Use the Kairos Circle to process feedback, learn from it, and take action. Whether the feedback is positive or negative, it's a chance to grow.

> Whether the feedback is positive or negative, **it's a chance to grow.**

- Frequency & Duration: Set up regular feedback cycles—weekly, bi-weekly, or monthly, depending on the needs of your team. Frequent, shorter feedback loops lead to faster course corrections and better performance.

The Leadership Pipeline in Action

When you implement the Leadership Pipeline, you create a self-sustaining engine of growth within your organization—a leadership engine. By continually recruiting, training, deploying, and reviewing your talent, you build a leadership engine that drives your company forward.

Imagine it like an engine where the cylinders are always pumping—recruiting new talent, training them for success, deploying them into the right roles, and continuously reviewing their progress. The result? A high-performing organization where leadership is always developing, and no one is left behind.

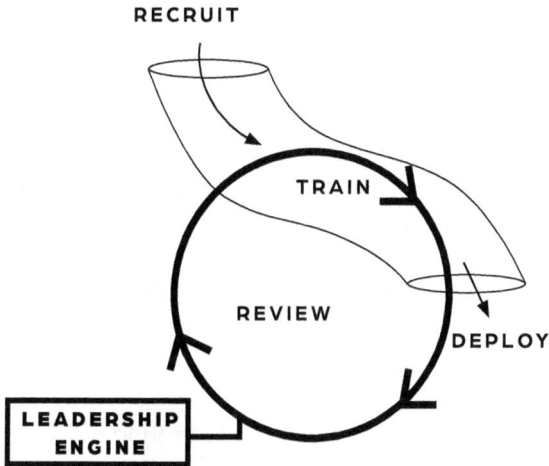

RECRUIT

TRAIN

REVIEW

DEPLOY

LEADERSHIP
ENGINE

TAKEAWAYS

- Recruit for character, capacity, chemistry, and competence: Get the right people on the bus by filtering for more than just technical skills.

- Train for both job-related skills and culture: Ensure your team knows how to perform their roles and how to operate within your company's values and culture.

- Deploy with clarity and growth in mind: Put the right people in the right roles and provide opportunities for continuous growth.

- Implement short feedback loops: Skip the annual reviews and create a culture of continuous improvement through regular, focused feedback.

- Build a leadership engine: By integrating the Leadership Pipeline, you create a self-sustaining system that continuously develops talent, ensuring your organization thrives for the long haul.

REFLECTION QUESTIONS

- How well are you recruiting for the four key areas—character, capacity, chemistry, and competence? Where can you improve your recruiting process to ensure you're getting the right people?

- Do you have a structured process for culture training in your organization? What steps can you take to ensure your team understands and operates according to your values?

- Are you deploying your people into roles that allow for growth and alignment? How can you create more opportunities for your team to stretch and develop?

- How often are you providing feedback to your team? What changes can you make to implement shorter feedback loops and more frequent course corrections?

- What steps can you take to start building your own leadership engine using the Leadership Pipeline? How will this impact your team's long-term success and your ability to scale your organization?

10

TRUST CODE

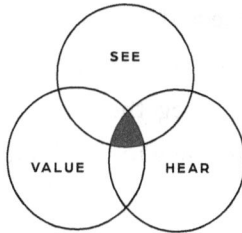

SEE

VALUE · HEAR

BUILD RELATIONSHIPS THAT
BUILD GREAT PARTNERSHIPS

There's a growing crisis in the culture of the workplace today: people feel disconnected. Many employees, regardless of age or role, describe their work environment as transactional, where the primary focus is on productivity and profits rather than relationships. In such environments, individuals often feel unimportant, rather than valued contributors to a greater purpose.

This lack of connection isn't just a productivity issue—it's a trust issue. Trust, the foundation of any thriving organization, is eroded when people don't feel seen, heard, or valued. Without trust, teams become fragmented, engagement plummets, and turnover rises. Organizations that fail to prioritize connection risk losing not only their people but also the collective energy and creativity that make success sustainable.

So, what's missing? Connection. In the rush to achieve goals and meet deadlines, it's all too easy to sideline the relationships that fuel trust. Yet, time and time again, research and experience show that connection is the cornerstone of trust—and trust is the glue that holds teams together. Without connection, even the most talented teams struggle to collaborate effectively, innovate, and navigate challenges.

Research and experience show that **connection is the cornerstone of trust.**

Instead of asking why people are disengaged or why teams struggle to work well together, what if we paused to reflect on how well we're fostering connection? This isn't about superficial gestures or team-building exercises; it's about creating a culture where people genuinely feel seen, heard, and valued. Isn't this just another Kairos moment—an invitation to examine how we're showing up as leaders and whether we're building environments where trust can thrive?

Here's the truth: people don't just want a paycheck or perks. They want to feel connected to their work, their colleagues, and their leaders. They want to know their contributions matter and that they belong. This need for connection isn't a modern luxury; it's a fundamental human requirement. Throughout history, humans have thrived in tribes—groups bound by common purpose, shared values, and mutual trust. Whether we acknowledge it or not, businesses function as tribes, and trust is the foundation that holds them together.

A tribe, simply defined, is a group of people linked by common ties—social, economic, or otherwise—who share a culture and work toward common goals. Within a tribe, every member knows they have a role to play, and they trust that others are equally committed to the shared vision. This trust doesn't happen by accident; it's built intentionally through consistent actions that prioritize connection.

So, the question is: Do your people feel like valued members of a tribe, or just another cog in the machine? Do they view your workplace as a community where they're seen, heard, and valued, or as a transactional space where output is prioritized over relationships?

Building trust begins with connection. When people feel connected—to their leaders, their colleagues, and the mission of their organization—they're more likely to trust, collaborate, and contribute their best. Connection fosters psychological safety, mutual respect, and a sense of belonging—all essential ingredients for trust.

In this chapter, we'll explore a simple framework for building trust by focusing on the three essential elements of connection: seeing, hearing, and valuing one another. Let's dive in.

Partnership = Risk

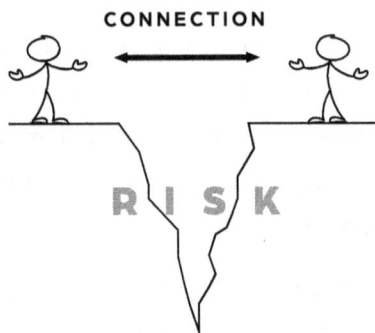

In all worthy endeavors, we must partner with others, and every successful partnership requires great attention to reciprocal trust. In the diagram above, we see this connection illustrated by the reciprocal arrows. It sounds simple, but why is building, maintaining, and repairing trust so difficult? Because trust requires us to entrust ourselves to others, and that always comes with risk. We all carry memories of trust being broken—whether intentional or not—which makes entrusting ourselves to others feel like a calculated gamble. And the reverse is true: others will also find it risky to trust us.

To overcome this reluctance, we must learn to build a **bridge of trust** with others. Stepping away from the safety of individualism and into partnership means risking potential pain, frustration, and loss. The strength of that trust bridge determines the weight of responsibility we can safely share with others. Building a culture of trust is imperative if we want to break the cycles of:

- siloing
- relational dysfunction

- isolation

- infighting

- unresolved conflict

- gossip

- and triangulation.

The **Trust Code** provides a simple framework to help our LOS resist the inevitable "bugs" that corrode our ability to work well together. One of the greatest challenges I encounter with the teams and companies I work with is distrust. Small infractions accumulate, leading to broken communication, fight-or-flight behaviors, and other dysfunctions. The Trust Code offers tools to repair those breaches, ensuring that *how* we work together doesn't undermine *what* we're trying to accomplish.

The Trust Code

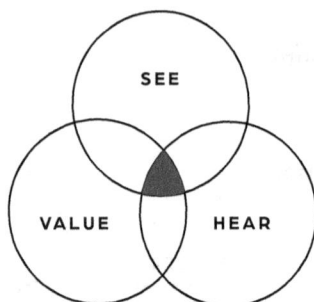

The Trust Code diagram highlights three essential elements to building the kind of trust that enables partnerships to bear greater weight and withstand more pressure. Let's explore these elements and how they can be practically applied:

SEE: The Eyes of Trust

You may be wondering, "What does "seeing" someone have to do with trust? Isn't it enough to get the job done without worrying about connection?" But here's the truth: trust starts with making others feel seen for who they are, not just for what they do. Seeing someone means recognizing their humanity beyond their role and demonstrating a baseline level of respect and appreciation for their individuality.

We work alongside people who are often vastly different from ourselves—different backgrounds, cultures, experiences, and personalities. Despite these differences, every person has an inherent need to feel *seen*. They need to know they are more than just a commodity. Prioritizing human connection lays the foundation for trust.

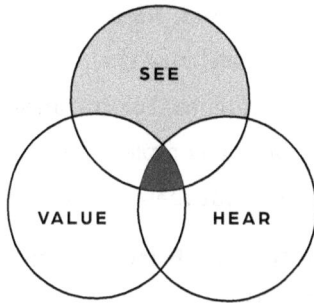

In any environment, whether at work or home, it's easy to sacrifice human decency in the name of productivity. But when we neglect connection, trust erodes. Many workplace conflicts stem from one or both parties feeling unseen. To see someone doesn't mean you have to agree with them, but it does mean handling them with respect, dignity, and honor—no matter their position.

Prioritizing human connection
lays the foundation for trust.

Practical Ways to See Others:

1. **Personal Recognition**: Take time to notice and acknowledge unique qualities, skills, or efforts. A simple "I see the hard work you put into this" can go a long way.

2. **Understand Their Story**: Invest in learning about their background, experiences, and aspirations. Ask open-ended questions like, "What motivates you?" or "What's something you're passionate about outside of work?"

3. **Recognize Non-Work Identities**: People are more than their job titles. Celebrate their life events, passions, and personal achievements. For instance, recognizing a team member's marathon completion or their child's graduation shows you care about them as a whole person.

4. **Adapt to Individual Needs**: Seeing someone also means understanding their unique preferences and challenges. Some people thrive on public recognition, while others value a private acknowledgment. Tailor your approach to the individual.

When people feel seen, they are more likely to trust and collaborate with you. They feel safe to bring their full selves to the table, fostering stronger connections and a more inclusive culture.

HEAR: The Heart of Trust

The second element of trust is the ability to truly hear others. Effective listening, as outlined in the EQ Matrix, involves active and reflective listening. It's not just about hearing words—it's about understanding what's being communicated, emotionally and intellectually.

Too often, conversations become battlegrounds where people focus more on what they're going to say next rather than practicing curiosity toward the other person. Miscommunication is common, especially in heated exchanges, and the only way to bridge this gap is to slow down, prioritize connection, and ask clarifying questions. Trust is built when the other person feels not only heard but understood.

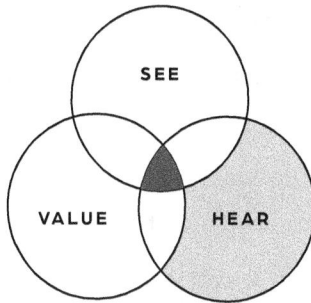

> Trust is built when the other person feels **not only heard but understood.**

Because humans are intellectual *and* emotional beings, dismissing emotions with phrases like "don't take it personally" is counterproductive. If someone's emotions are disrupted, their ability to think rationally is compromised. By giving them space to acknowledge their feelings, we help them regain their composure and clarity. Remember, if we can't own our emotions, they will own us. Listening is not just about what someone thinks but also about what they feel.

Practical Ways to Hear Others:

1. Active Listening Techniques:

- Maintain eye contact to signal attention.
- Nod or use brief verbal affirmations like "I see," "Go on," or "That makes sense."
- Avoid distractions like checking your phone or interrupting.

2. Reflective Listening:

- Paraphrase what they've said to ensure understanding: "What I hear you saying is..."

- Validate emotions, even if you disagree with the content: "I can see why that might feel frustrating."

3. Ask Clarifying Questions: Dive deeper by asking, "Can you elaborate on that?" or "What do you think would help resolve this?"

4. Pay Attention to Non-Verbal Cues: Tone, posture, and facial expressions often reveal what words don't. If you notice tension or hesitation, acknowledge it gently: "You seem a bit hesitant. Is there something else on your mind?"

When people feel heard, they experience psychological safety. They're more likely to share ideas, voice concerns, and engage in problem-solving. This transparency strengthens relationships and improves team dynamics.

When people feel heard, they experience psychological safety.

VALUE: The Hands of Trust

The third element, *value*, is about serving others in ways that communicate their worth. As leaders, it's our responsibility to leverage our time, energy, and resources to serve those we work with. When we actively seek opportunities to support others, we send a clear message: "You matter." Conversely, withholding support undermines trust.

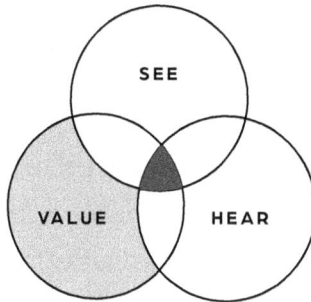

Gary Chapman's *The Five Love Languages* provides a useful lens for understanding how to demonstrate value: words of affirmation, quality time, acts of service, gifts, and physical touch (appropriately applied). While not all of these apply to the workplace, they highlight the importance of tailoring our efforts to meet the unique needs of those we serve. Wise leaders understand that meeting others where they are fosters a reciprocal sense of trust and commitment.

Practical Ways to Value Others:

1. **Invest Time and Resources**: Show you value someone by providing opportunities for growth, such as training programs, mentorship, or tools to succeed in their role.

2. **Express Appreciation Frequently**: Don't wait for performance reviews to recognize someone's contributions. A

quick email, a handwritten note, or a public shout-out can make a lasting impression.

3. **Serve Without Strings Attached**: Genuine service communicates trust and respect. Ask, "How can I support you?" and then follow through without expecting anything in return.

4. **Advocate for Them**: Whether in meetings, promotions, or other opportunities, use your position to highlight their strengths and create opportunities for advancement.

5. **Respect Their Boundaries**: Valuing someone also means honoring their limits and personal space. Respect their time, energy, and individuality.

When people feel valued, they're more engaged, motivated, and committed to the team or organization. They're also more likely to reciprocate, creating a cycle of mutual trust and collaboration.

When people feel valued, they're more engaged, motivated, and committed to the team or organization.

Leaders Go First

Let me emphasize: leaders go first. It's tempting to think, *I'll give when they give*, but maturing leaders recognize their role as cultural architects. They know it's their responsibility to define the culture through their example, rather than waiting for others to step up.

I once heard a wise woman say, "Great relationships aren't 50/50. They're 100/100." This means that both parties in a partnership are fully responsible for bringing their best to the table. Anytime I experience a gap in connection between me and my spouse, kids, or colleagues, I start by reflecting on whether I've failed to effectively communicate *seeing*, *hearing*, or *valuing* them. And because I'm committed to leading in every area of my life, I fight to go first.

Creating a culture where everyone feels seen, heard and valued is paramount to building a great business. People are your most valuable asset and treating them so will reap incredible dividends. Our responsibility as leaders is to embody these values, model them continuously and expect that others will follow.

People are your most valuable asset and treating them so will reap incredible dividends.

KEY TAKEAWAYS

- Trust is the foundation of every successful relationship in the workplace. When employees feel seen, heard, and valued, collaboration flourishes, and productivity increases. Without trust, teams become fragmented, engagement diminishes, and organizational success suffers.

- Trusting others—and being trusted in return—always involves risk. Building trust requires vulnerability and a willingness to entrust others with responsibilities, knowing there is always a chance of disappointment. However, this risk is essential for creating strong, collaborative partnerships.

- Building trust involves three essential actions:
  - **See:** Recognizing people for who they are beyond their roles.
  - **Hear:** Practicing active and reflective listening to understand both thoughts and feelings.
  - **Value:** Demonstrating appreciation and respect through support, recognition, and advocacy.

- Leaders have the responsibility to go first in fostering trust. By embodying the principles of seeing, hearing, and valuing others, leaders model the behaviors they expect from their teams, setting the tone for a culture of trust and collaboration.

When people feel connected to their leaders, colleagues, and mission, they are more likely to engage fully and contribute their best efforts. A strong sense of belonging empowers individuals to take risks, share ideas, and collaborate effectively.

REFLECTION QUESTIONS

- Do your team members feel seen, heard, and valued in your organization? How do you currently foster genuine connections with your team?

- Reflect on a time when you struggled to trust a colleague or team member. What barriers prevented trust from forming? What specific actions can you take to rebuild trust with a colleague or team member who feels disconnected?

- How are you modeling the principles of seeing, hearing, and valuing others in your daily leadership practices?

- What risks have you taken recently to build or strengthen trust within your organization? Are you creating an environment where others feel safe taking similar risks?

- Does your organizational culture prioritize trust and connection, or is it more focused on productivity and output? How can you reshape your leadership practices to emphasize the importance of trust without compromising results?

11

THE PRODUCTIVITY PENDULUM

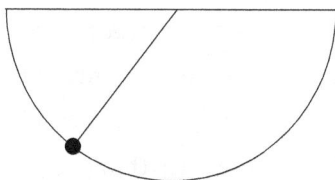

ENGAGE HEALTHY RHYTHMS FOR
SUSTAINABLE OUTPUT

Everywhere you look in the natural world, you see incredible expressions of ingenuity, productivity, and fruitfulness. Think about ants and bees collaborating in astonishingly large numbers to build nests, protect their queen, forage for sustenance, and ward off threats. Or consider a single tree that disperses thousands of seeds each year, populating its environment with homes and food for countless creatures, including humans. Killer whales—often called "wolves of the sea"—hunt together using sophisticated tactics, travel in large pods, and communicate through highly developed methods. The sheer quality and quantity of output in nature is breathtaking. It's almost as if the world never sleeps.

Yet all this productivity is not the result of constant activity. Nature thrives on rhythms—discernible cycles of rest and work, retreat and engagement, sleep and movement. Like the steady tick-tock of a metronome, life flourishes through the pendulum-like swing between times of activity and pause. Human beings, like the rest of nature, were designed to thrive when we honor these rhythms. Sustainable output depends on these rhythms.

> **Nature thrives on rhythms—** discernible cycles of rest and work, retreat and engagement, sleep and movement.

Think about it: we sleep for roughly one-third of our lives—about 229,961 hours in a lifetime. That's approximately 33 years spent in bed! While we may try to cheat some of that time with late-night work or entertainment, sleep is essential for health and vitality. It's a daily rhythm we can't escape. The same is true of other natural rhythms, like eating, drinking water, or breathing. These rhythms are nonnegotiable, and when we ignore them, our bodies and minds remind us—through fatigue, sickness, disorientation, or burnout—that we cannot override our design.

We often make the mistake of seeing the goal of life as *resting from our work*. The truth is, we are sustainably more productive when we embrace a *work from rest* mindset. This is the foundation of sustainable productivity and well-being. When we honor these rhythms, we unlock greater energy, focus, and resilience—allowing us to operate at our best.

The Productivity Pendulum

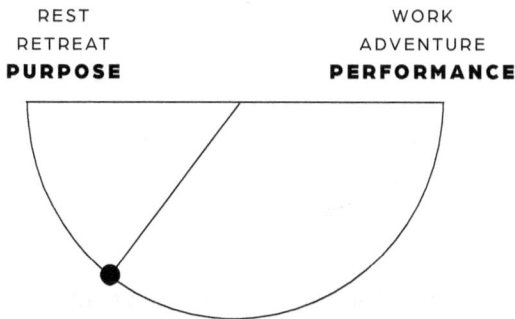

REST
RETREAT
PURPOSE

WORK
ADVENTURE
PERFORMANCE

The pendulum swing in the diagram above illustrates the tension we all feel as we try to live in harmony with ourselves and the world around us. The health of our bodies, relationships, and work depends on our willingness to honor the balance between rest and work, retreat and adventure, and purpose and performance.

Too often, however, our desire for achievement drives us to deny our natural rhythms. We push the pendulum further and further to the right, overworking ourselves in the name of productivity. We keep pushing—until we find ourselves exhausted and burned out.

When this happens, weekends become a time to crash rather than reset, and we collapse into bed at night, dreading the alarm clock that signals another grueling day ahead. This "rest from work" mentality is a cultural deception that values us more as

EXHAUSTION
BURNOUT

REST
RETREAT
PURPOSE

WORK
ADVENTURE
PERFORMANCE

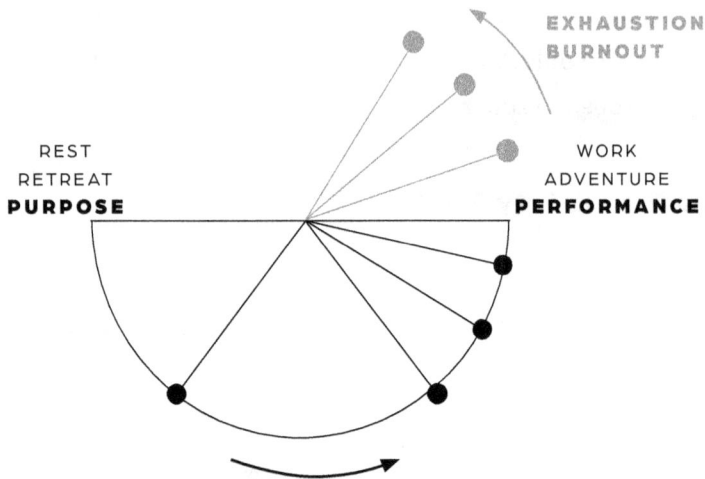

human doings than *human beings*. It tells us that our worth is tied to our productivity, not our personhood.

Ironically, by ignoring the rhythms of rest, we diminish the quality of our work. We've all been there—showing up to meetings half-asleep, snapping at loved ones, or struggling to focus—because we didn't prioritize rest. Sometimes, disruptions to our rhythms are unavoidable (like young children, illness, or jet lag). But neglecting these rhythms should be the exception, not the rule.

We must learn to view rest as a priority, not an afterthought. After all, we can only give to others what we first invest in ourselves. Like a car that keeps running even after the warning light comes on, our bodies and minds are resilient, but they have limits. I've worked with too many leaders who ignored those limits until it was too late—sacrificing their health, relationships, and careers to burnout.

If our output is determined by our input, then we must pay more attention to how we care for ourselves. The world deserves a well-rested, nourished, clear-minded, and energized version of you. Unlike a machine, you cannot run 24/7. You must shut down to recharge and reset. When you adopt a "work from rest" mindset, you'll find yourself operating with clarity and sustainable energy, which leads to increased productivity and fulfillment.

If our output is determined by our input, then **we must pay more attention to how we care for ourselves.**

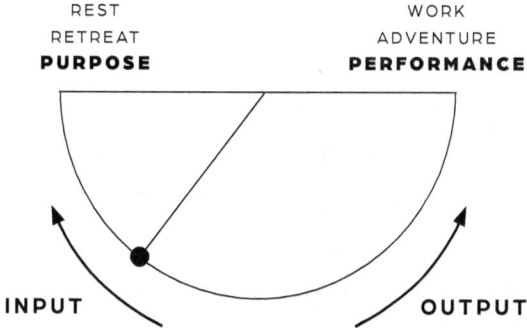

REST
RETREAT
PURPOSE

WORK
ADVENTURE
PERFORMANCE

INPUT

OUTPUT

Input – Cultivating Rest & Purpose

Without healthy rhythms of rest, maintenance, and retreat, we lose connection with who we are and how we want to operate. Going back to the *EQ Matrix,* we live best from the inside out, cultivating within ourselves the qualities we want to make available to others. Without this intentional input, we risk running on empty, which inevitably undermines our ability to lead effectively. There are five key areas of input we must nurture if we want to lead powerfully and sustainably:

```
           REST                    WORK
         RETREAT                 ADVENTURE
         PURPOSE                 PERFORMANCE
```

- PERSONHOOD
- PERSPECTIVE
- PRIORITIES
- POWER
- PLAY

Personhood

Personhood is about who you are before you've done anything. It's your identity, self-perception, and sense of worth apart from any accomplishments. When your personhood is tied to what you do, your sense of self becomes fragile, precariously shaped by the highs and lows of success and failure. In this state, you find yourself working to prove your value, rather than operating from a place of intrinsic self-worth.

When we allow our identity to be determined by what we achieve, we end up on a relentless treadmill of acceptance and approval. In this mindset, you're only as valuable as your last performance. Over time, this leads to burnout, depression, materialism, and identity crisis. Whether I'm working with professional athletes, CEOs, or crypto millionaires, I've seen how the pressure to "earn" one's worth ultimately takes its toll.

It is crucial to establish your personhood before stepping into the demands of the world. In the quiet spaces of your internal world, you have the opportunity to define who you are, what you value, and what you stand for. This is where purpose begins. While it's true that our parents often set the stage for this in our younger years, as adults, it becomes our responsibility to take that space for ourselves. If we don't, the world will shape us instead—usually in ways that do not serve us.

Your personhood is best reflected in your *I am* statements. I am smart. I am loved. I am funny. I am creative. I am hardworking. Take a moment and reflect on what you most often say to yourself. It's one thing to be honest about your shortcomings, but another to self-deprecate. The only *I am* statements you should entertain are those which genuinely reflect who you are and that empower you to be so.

Perspective

I've heard it said, "We see the world not as it is, but as we are." Perspective shapes how we interpret and respond to everything we encounter. It's not the facts of a situation that define us, but how we perceive and process them.

Life comes at us quickly, and it's easy to become reactive rather than reflective. Without an intentional pause, we risk allowing emotions or misinterpretations to cloud our judgment. Taking time to reflect creates space to process emotions, understand situations more clearly, and determine the best course of action. This is where reframing becomes an invaluable tool.

> **Reframing starts with remembering that life is not happening to you, but for you.**

Reframing starts with remembering that life is not happening *to* you, but *for* you. When we shift our perspective from fear, insecurity, or self-protection to hope and opportunity, we take back control of our narrative. Life is hard—there's no disputing that—but adopting a victim or villain mindset only makes it harder. Choosing to reframe challenges into opportunities empowers us to face them with strength and clarity.

Priorities

Healthy rhythms of rest give us the time and clarity needed to recalibrate our priorities. In today's world, where technology provides constant access to information and communication, it's easy to fall prey to the tyranny of the urgent. Without regular reflection, we can lose sight of what truly matters.

When we take the time to reconnect with our personhood and perspective, we become better equipped to set and maintain priorities that align with our values. It's important to remember that we are finite beings with limited time, energy, and resources. Every "yes" we give to one thing is a "no" to something else. We cannot do everything, and trying to do so inevitably leads to frustration and exhaustion.

Prioritization is an expression of purpose. If you want to know what truly matters to someone, look at how they invest their time, energy, and resources. In the same way that a bank statement reveals our financial priorities, our calendars reveal our life priorities.

Prioritization is an expression of purpose.

We must regularly center ourselves, evaluate our purpose, and align our priorities across every area of life to ensure we're moving in a direction that leads to the greatest satisfaction and fulfillment. Human beings thrive when living with purpose; human doings get stuck in cycles of aimless activity.

Power

Rest, rejuvenation, and self-connection are the well springs for your personal power. By power, I am referring to what makes you unique, special, one-of-a-kind. Too easily we compare ourselves to others, wishing we could be like someone else. Just remember, there is no one else like you on planet earth. You have a distinct fingerprint, a special purpose for existing, and there will never be another *you* again! Only you can have the influence and impact that you are capable of.

This is why it's so important to pay attention to our attitudes, behaviors, and decisions. Just like a phone that must be charged overnight to function properly the next day, we must identify and honor the inputs we need to stay fully charged and powered.

Without this intentionality, we risk becoming depleted and ineffective, unable to serve ourselves or others.

The purpose of the MPWR LOS Toolkit is to help you unlock your leadership potential and harness your power. The question is, how will you use that power? Will you wield it selfishly or for the benefit of others? Will you neglect it, or will you cultivate it to give the world the best version of yourself?

Play

In the fast-paced, achievement-driven culture we inhabit, *play* often gets relegated to childhood, seen as a luxury rather than a necessity. But the truth is, play is a critical input for personal and professional health—one that fuels creativity, strengthens relationships, and revitalizes our energy. Play allows us to step outside the confines of structured productivity and reconnect with joy, curiosity, and spontaneity. Whether it's a game of basketball, experimenting with a new hobby, or simply laughing with friends, play reminds us that life isn't just about what we accomplish but also about the joy we experience along the way.

Neuroscience backs this up. Engaging in playful activities activates the brain's reward system, reduces stress, and improves problem-solving skills. Play serves as a mental reset, helping us approach challenges with a fresh perspective. It also fosters connection with others—sharing in moments of play builds trust, camaraderie, and a sense of belonging. Leaders who prioritize play not only experience the benefits themselves but also create a

Play is not a distraction from serious work; it is a vital rhythm that enhances our ability to show up with clarity, focus, and innovation.

culture where teams feel energized, creative, and connected. Play is not a distraction from serious work; it is a vital rhythm that enhances our ability to show up with clarity, focus, and innovation.

Integrating play as an input is about reclaiming balance in our lives. It's not something we earn after hard work—it's a necessary rhythm that fuels the work itself. When we embrace play as a critical input, we remind ourselves that leadership is not just about achieving goals but also about enjoying the journey and bringing others along for the ride.

By honoring these areas of input—personhood, perspective, priorities, power and play—you build a strong foundation for effective and sustainable leadership. These rhythms remind us that the measure of our input determines the quality of our output. It's not selfish to invest in yourself; it's essential to be the leader your world needs.

Predictable Patterns: Daily, Weekly, and Seasonal Rhythms

To maintain the balance of the Productivity Pendulum, we need predictable patterns of rest and work. These patterns are like rituals that ground us, providing structure and ensuring that we're constantly recharging.

Daily Rhythms

Daily rhythms might include sleep patterns, exercise routines, or how you manage your emails. These habits may seem small, but over time, they shape your entire life.

Reflection Questions:

- What daily habits are helping you stay balanced?
- Are there any that need to be recalibrated or eliminated?

Weekly Rhythms

These could be things like family dinners, team meetings, or taking time to reflect on the past week. Weekly rhythms give you a chance to reset and recalibrate, ensuring you stay aligned with your goals.

Reflection Questions:

- What weekly patterns are serving your life and work?
- Are there any changes you need to make to better align with your priorities?

Seasonal Rhythms

Seasonal rhythms are larger patterns—like vacations, quarterly reviews, or leadership retreats. These provide an opportunity for deep rest and reflection, allowing you to step back and see the bigger picture.

Reflection Questions:

- Do you plan your seasonal rhythms, or do they sneak up on you?

- How can you be more intentional about scheduling these periods of rest and reflection?

TAKEAWAYS

- The Productivity Pendulum swings between input (rest, retreat, reflection) and output (work, achievement, productivity).

- You're not designed to work constantly. Embracing rest isn't a luxury—it's a necessity.

- To be truly productive, you need to develop predictable patterns of rest and work at daily, weekly, and seasonal levels.

- Your greatest power comes from working from rest, not just crashing into it.

REFLECTION QUESTIONS

- Do you currently live with a work from rest or a rest from work mentality?

- How well are you maintaining balance in your daily, weekly, and seasonal rhythms?

- What steps can you take to recalibrate your input (rest, reflection, retreat) so that you can increase your output?

- Where in your life are you pushing the pendulum too far toward work, and what can you do to bring it back into balance?

12

---

5 CAPITALS

---

5 CAPITALS

- VISION
- RELATIONAL
- PHYSICAL
- INTELLECTUAL
- FINANCIAL

INVEST IN A LIFE THAT MATTERS

How often have we sacrificed one value on the altar of another, only to realize later that we made the wrong trade? Maybe we worked late for months on end, only to see the strain it put on our home life. Perhaps we gave up exercise or sleep to pour extra effort into a work project. I've seen leaders climb the ladder of promotion while jeopardizing relationships with coworkers, and I've watched people abandon their dreams in favor of immediate security and stability. Here's the hard question: did the ends justify the means in those scenarios? At the time, we must have thought so, or we wouldn't have made the sacrifice. But all too often, it's only when the consequences of those trade-offs catch up to us that we realize the cost of our decisions.

The MPWR LOS must include a tool that helps us navigate these inevitable trade-offs with greater clarity and purpose. Every "yes" to one thing is a "no" to something else. Sometimes these trade-offs are clear; other times, they're harder to discern. Either way, having a clear view of the sacrifices we're making—and ensuring they align with our values—gives us the best chance of making decisions that lead to long-term fulfillment.

Of course, there will be times when we sacrifice time with our families to finish an important project, miss a workout to spend more time with loved ones, or grab fast food because we're in a rush. The issue isn't the occasional trade-off; it's how easy it is to make these sacrifices repeatedly without recognizing the cumulative impact on our lives. Over time, the wrong trade-offs can derail us from living a life that truly matters.

Over time, the wrong trade-offs can **derail us from living a life that truly matters.**

It's helpful to remember that we are finite beings managing finite resources. This is why it's useful to think of life as an investment strategy. Each day, we make decisions about how to invest our time, energy, and resources with the hope of achieving a meaningful return on investment (ROI). I take my wife on date nights and vacations to invest in our marriage. I hit the gym five times a week to build strength and endurance for life's demands. Our family makes regular financial investments to prepare for retirement and our children's futures. I meet weekly with my core team to develop relational continuity and ensure we stay on track to meet our goals. And I get out on the golf course a couple of times each week to invest in my own well-being.

How we allocate our time, energy, and resources is much like managing a financial budget. Without clear goals, boundaries, and accountability, we're unlikely to end up where we want to be. This is where the **5 Capitals Tool** comes in—a framework designed to help us evaluate our key resources and align our investments with what truly matters. By adopting this perspective, we can approach life with intentionality, ensuring that the ROI on our investments reflects the life we desire to build.

The 5 Capitals

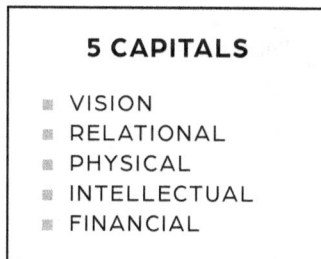

```
5 CAPITALS

■ VISION
■ RELATIONAL
■ PHYSICAL
■ INTELLECTUAL
■ FINANCIAL
```

The 5 Capitals are like the five main bank accounts you have in life. These capitals represent key areas where we invest our time, energy, and resources every day. Whether we're aware of it or not, every decision we make involves trading one capital for another. The question is: are you making the right trades?

Here are the five capitals:

- **Vision Capital**: Clarity on what gives your life significance, meaning and purpose

- **Relational Capital**: The strength of your relationships and the trust you've built with others

- **Physical Capital**: Your time, energy, and physical well-being

- **Intellectual Capital**: What you know and the skills you've developed

- **Financial Capital**: The cash and assets you've accumulated

In the table below we see each capital and the currencies we're trading for each account.

CAPITAL	CURRENCIES
VISION	SIGNIFICANCE, MEANING & PURPOSE
RELATIONAL	FRIENDS & FAMILY
PHYSICAL	TIME & ENERGY
INTELLECTUAL	KNOWLEDGE & KNOW-HOW
FINANCIAL	CASH & ASSETS

In life, we're constantly investing with and for these five capitals, sometimes intentionally, sometimes unconsciously. The key to living a life of purpose and satisfaction is knowing how to value these capitals, how to prioritize their growth when needed, and how to invest wisely for our desired ROI.

Defining the 5 Capitals

Vision Capital

Vision Capital is measured by the clarity we have about what gives our lives significance and purpose. While each of us may draw our purpose from different worldviews, every person is hardwired to thrive when deeply connected to what provides a sense of belonging and meaning. In my experience, people are most satisfied with their Vision Capital when it is closely tied to two elements: **1) intimate connection with their tribe or community** and **2) serving the world in a meaningful way.**

Vision Capital serves as our **North Star**—the conviction that guides why we exist and informs how we live. It shapes how we invest our other capitals and provides us with peace even in the face of hardship. The challenge is maintaining a balanced perspective about the value of our lives.

> Vision Capital serves as our **North Star.**

Sometimes we overestimate our importance, acting as though the world revolves around us, only to forget that we'll eventually fade from memory after we're gone. Other times, we underestimate our impact, losing sight of the incredible legacy our life investments create. For example, my great-grandchildren may know very little about who I am, but the way I invest in my children today will have a profound and lasting influence on their lives.

Vision Capital allows us to align our daily actions with a higher purpose, ensuring that how we live and invest our resources reflects what matters most. It reminds us that our lives are part of a larger story—one that stretches beyond us to impact others in ways we may never fully see.

Questions:

1. Do you have a clear sense of your purpose?

2. Does your vision for your life guide your daily decisions?

3. How often do you reconnect with what really matters to you?

Relational Capital

Relational Capital represents the strength of your relationships, measured by the deposits you've made over time and your ability to make withdrawals when needed. In simple terms, it reflects the trust you've built with family, friends, colleagues, and others in your life. Relational Capital can also be assessed through the lens of the **Trust Code**, where the quality of trust determines the strength of any relationship. In this way, the stronger the trust, the greater your Relational Capital.

When I've made more withdrawals than deposits with my wife—perhaps by neglecting quality time or not showing appreciation—my Relational Capital with her decreases. The same is true with clients. If I've failed to check in regularly or mishandled a situation (yes, it happens!), my capital with them diminishes. Conversely, when I make intentional investments—whether it's time, energy, or other capitals—my Relational Capital grows. The stronger my investment, the stronger the relationship.

To grow my Relational Capital, I use the diagram below to help prioritize investments in the right relationships. It's all too easy to focus on outer-circle connections, like work colleagues or acquaintances, at the expense of those in our inner circles—our partners, family, and closest friends. We've all been guilty of neglecting these more valuable relationships under the pressures of deadlines or distractions. But the best practice is to consistently prioritize the relationships that matter most, ensuring we're investing the time, energy, and trust that create enduring connections.

The best practice is to consistently **prioritize the relationships that matter most.**

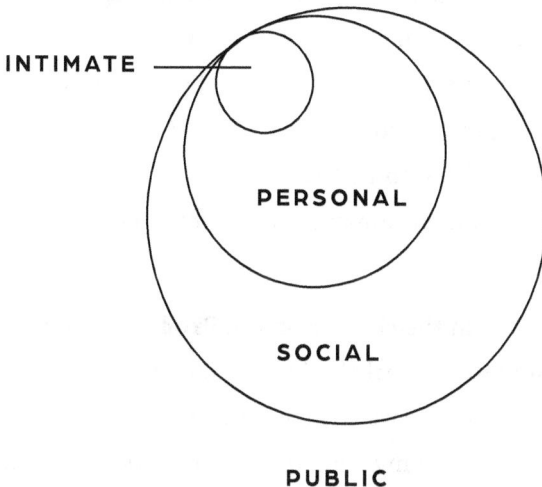

INTIMATE

PERSONAL

SOCIAL

PUBLIC

Questions:

1. Are you investing in the relationships that matter most? How so?

2. Are you making regular deposits, or are you draining your Relational Capital?

3. Where could you better prioritize your more important relationships?

Physical Capital

Physical Capital is measured by two key resources: your time and your energy. Everyone has the same 24 hours in a day and seven days in a week, but not everyone stewards that time effectively. Similarly, while energy levels can be influenced by many factors, they are directly impacted by how well we manage three foundational areas: **sleep, exercise, and nutrition**. When we are intentional about taking care of our physical bodies, our energy levels increase, equipping us to maximize our effectiveness. With the technologies available to us today, there's no reason not to have a clear strategy for optimizing these areas and sustaining high energy levels.

As discussed in the chapter on the **Productivity Pendulum**, our calendars often reveal the investment strategy for our time. For years, I've made it a weekly habit to study my calendar, reflecting on how I invested my time the previous week and the ROI it yielded. This process also helps me determine the most strategic investments for the week ahead. When our kids were younger, my wife and I reviewed our calendars together each week to ensure we were aligned on how we were investing our time as a family. This practice helped us prioritize the activities that mattered most and ensure our collective time and energy were yielding the greatest returns for our family's goals and values.

Questions:

1. How clear and confident are you that your calendar reflects your key priorities? How so?

2. Are you treating sleep, exercise, and nutrition as essentials or as options?

3. What changes could you make to maximize your Physical Capital?

Intellectual Capital

Intellectual Capital represents two key assets: **what we know** and **what we know how to do**—otherwise known as knowledge and know-how. While these two components are closely related, they are not the same. **Knowledge** is the information, theories, and insights we acquire through learning, reading, or studying. It's what fills our minds and expands our understanding of the world. **Know-how**, on the other hand, is the practical application of that knowledge—the ability to translate what we've learned into real-world action and results.

The distinction between knowledge and know-how is crucial. For example, you might read every book on leadership and know the theory inside and out but applying that knowledge in the heat of a difficult team meeting is a different skill altogether. Similarly, understanding the mechanics of a golf swing doesn't guarantee you can hit a golf ball effectively. True Intellectual Capital grows when we bridge the gap between knowledge and know-how, turning insights into skills that deliver tangible results.

True Intellectual Capital grows **when we bridge the gap between knowledge and know-how.**

Life constantly presents us with opportunities to expand both knowledge and know-how. However, gaining new know-how often requires stepping into the role of a learner, embracing the discomfort of unfamiliar territory. This is where the **Development Square** comes in. By understanding how the development process works, we can approach learning with humility and patience, recognizing that growth—especially in know-how—takes practice, feedback, and perseverance.

Leaders who prioritize the growth of their Intellectual Capital become invaluable to their teams and organizations. They demonstrate the ability to adapt to new challenges, model a commitment to lifelong learning, and empower others to do the same. When we actively pursue both knowledge and know-how, we not only enrich our own lives but also enhance our ability to serve others and make meaningful contributions in every area of life.

Questions:

1. What areas of knowledge or skill do you need to invest in right now?

2. Are you applying the Intellectual Capital you already have effectively?

3. Where are you most tempted to leverage knowledge when what you really need is know-how?

Financial Capital

Financial Capital is the most tangible of the Five Capitals, measured in cash, savings, investments, and physical assets. These assets might include homes, cars, retirement accounts, stocks, bonds, or even luxury items like boats and private planes. Financial Capital is what most people immediately think of when they hear the word "capital," as it's central to how we navigate our material needs and goals. However, its importance goes far beyond mere accumulation.

Financial Capital represents both a means and an opportunity—it's the fuel that empowers us to invest in other areas of life. When managed wisely, it can serve as a tool to amplify our **Vision Capital** by funding endeavors aligned with our purpose, support our **Relational Capital** through family vacations or meaningful experiences, and even enhance our **Physical Capital** through investments in health, wellness, and rest. But when mismanaged or viewed as an end in itself, Financial Capital can become a source of stress, division, and misplaced priorities.

The key to building and sustaining Financial Capital is understanding that it's not just about how much you earn, but how you manage, allocate, and invest it. This requires clarity around your goals and values. For example, if family is one of your core values, your spending and saving habits should reflect that—whether through budgeting for quality time together, saving for a child's education, or ensuring financial security for your household. If health and vitality are priorities, it might mean investing in gym memberships, nutrition coaching, or high-quality food. Financial Capital becomes most meaningful when it is strategically aligned with what truly matters in your life.

Expanding your Financial Capital is not just about increasing income but also leveraging it effectively. This includes saving for long-term goals, building diverse investments, and ensuring you're prepared for unexpected challenges through emergency funds or insurance. Wealth-building is a long game, and it requires discipline, intentionality, and sometimes sacrifice.

Ultimately, Financial Capital is a tool. It's a resource that can support a life of purpose and impact if we manage it with intention. But it's also a reflection of our values—how we save, spend, and invest speaks volumes about what we prioritize. By aligning our financial decisions with the other capitals, we can ensure that our Financial Capital serves a greater purpose, contributing to a legacy that extends well beyond ourselves.

Financial Capital is a tool. It's a resource that can support a life of purpose and impact if we manage it with intention.

Questions:

1. How are you managing your financial resources?

2. Are you clear on your financial goals?

3. How does your Financial Capital support your overall life vision?

Capital Valuation

Now that we understand each of the 5 Capitals, we must reflect on how we value them relative to one another. Take a moment to consider the prevailing culture in the United States. How would you order the 5 Capitals from most to least valuable to reflect this mindset?

In our traditional academic system, social media, and entertainment industry, it's no surprise that financial and intellectual status are often viewed as the most important. From a young age, we're told to prioritize education to secure high-paying careers. Society idolizes celebrities and successful entrepreneurs because they seem to "have it all." We endlessly consume tabloid gossip and marvel at their luxurious lifestyles, secretly wishing we could trade places with them. Yet, we often fail to recognize that money and degrees can't buy healthy relationships, purpose, or inner peace. If wealth and fame were the ultimate measures of fulfillment, Hollywood would be the happiest place on Earth.

That's not to say money isn't important—it absolutely is. Financial Capital is necessary for stability, opportunity, and achieving life goals. But it isn't more valuable than Vision or Relational

Capital, which bring deeper meaning to our lives.

Now, take a moment to reflect on your personal ranking of the 5 Capitals. Is it different from the cultural norm? If so, why? There's no single "correct" order, but in my experience working with some of the most effective leaders, they tend to agree on this hierarchy: Vision, Relational, Physical, Intellectual, Financial. Many of these leaders are in the second half of their lives, which often brings a broader and more thoughtful perspective about what matters most.

Consider this: What good is financial wealth without the wisdom to manage it? Many lottery winners and retired athletes go bankrupt because they lack the Intellectual Capital to invest or save for the long term. Similarly, what value is money or advanced degrees if you're physically unwell and lack the energy to enjoy your success? History is full of brilliant, wealthy people who would have traded everything for restored health or a loving family.

Though all 5 Capitals are valuable, they are not equally valuable. I've seen—and experienced myself—the pain of trading higher capitals for lesser ones. It's a steep price to pay. No amount of money can replace critical relationships, physical health, or peace of mind. What helps us avoid these short-sighted trade-offs is Vision Capital. When we have a clear sense of purpose, we make better decisions and invest in what truly matters.

In my book, *Transform Your Trajectory*, I share a story of how I nearly lost my marriage because I lost sight of my Vision Capital. I spent too many years sacrificing my relationship with my wife and children to grow my business and indulge in unhealthy habits. At the time, these trade-offs didn't seem problematic—but hindsight revealed the true cost. That's why staying connected to our Vision Capital is critical. It provides the compass we need to navigate life's complexities, ensuring our investments align with the legacy we want to leave behind.

Questions:

1. What does your current capital ranking look like?

2. Are you valuing one capital too highly at the expense of others?

3. What changes could you make to your capital investments?

Assessing Your Capitals

Just as we can open up our bank accounts to see our financial standing, we need to regularly assess the state of our *5 Capital accounts*. Are we thriving in certain areas, or are there accounts running on empty? Taking stock of where we stand helps us make informed decisions about where and how to invest. For each of the Capitals below, take a moment to reflect and rate yourself on a scale of 1 to 10 (10 = rich, 1 = poor). Remember, this evaluation is personal—it's about how you perceive your own life, not how you compare yourself to others.

As you score each account, try to be honest without judgment. Think of this exercise as a financial audit for your life—it's a tool to gain clarity, not a reason to criticize yourself. Every one of us has areas of strength and areas needing more attention. The goal is to identify opportunities for recalibration.

CAPITAL	CURRENCIES	SCORE
VISION	SIGNIFICANCE, MEANING & PURPOSE	
RELATIONAL	FRIENDS & FAMILY	
PHYSICAL	TIME & ENERGY	
INTELLECTUAL	KNOWLEDGE & KNOW-HOW	
FINANCIAL	CASH & ASSETS	

Wherever your scores fall, the good news is that *it's never too late to recalibrate your investment strategy.* Life is dynamic, and so are our circumstances. As these circumstances shift, so too must our approach to how we spend our time, energy, and resources. A season of parenting young children, for instance, may naturally require greater investments in Relational and Physical Capital, while another season might allow more focus on Intellectual or Financial Capital. The key is maintaining a value-driven order that keeps your investments aligned with your long-term vision and priorities.

By consistently reassessing and realigning your investments, you ensure that your resources are working for you—not against you. A thoughtful, intentional approach to your 5 Capitals will yield a desirable ROI over time, helping you live a life of fulfillment, purpose, and balance.

Questions:

1. Were you surprised by how you scored yourself?

2. Which capital do you feel is the strongest?

3. Which one needs the most investment?

Your Investment Strategy

There are two foundational rules to consider when crafting your investment strategy:

1. To grow one capital, you must invest the other four.

2. It's always in your best interest to trade less valuable capitals for more valuable ones.

If you want to grow one of the 5 Capitals, you need to leverage the others. For example, improving your fitness requires more than just showing up at the gym. You'll benefit from a clear vision of *why* this goal matters, support from friends or a community, intentional time and energy set aside, and perhaps a financial investment in a trainer or membership. Similarly, if you want to increase your financial outlook, you'll need a purposeful vision for what the money is for, relational connections with those who can mentor you, time and energy to learn and apply new skills, and possibly a financial investment in education or resources.

> **Trading less valuable capitals for more valuable ones is** always a smart move.

Trading less valuable capitals for more valuable ones is always a smart move. Why?

1. Life becomes more meaningful and fulfilling when you prioritize Vision, Relational, and Physical Capitals—especially as you age and realize these are the ones that matter most in the long run.

2. Once these capitals are thriving, they allow you to enjoy the lesser capitals more fully.

For example, early in our nonprofit leadership days, we didn't earn much, but we cultivated strong relationships that opened doors to incredible experiences: vacations in Alaska, bucket-list golf courses, luxurious retreats, and fine dining we could never have afforded on our salaries. These were all made possible because we prioritized Relational Capital, which we later traded for enjoyable but less valuable financial or experiential rewards.

In my coaching business, I regularly expand my Intellectual Capital by learning about new industries from my clients. They generously share their expertise because of the relational equity I've already invested in them.

Remember, we're trading capitals every day, whether we realize it or not. How you treat your family before heading to work, delegating chores to your kids, buying your morning coffee, or staying late to help your boss are all part of an ongoing investment strategy. The key question is whether you're trading with intention and aiming for a clear return on investment (ROI). The clearer your desired outcome, the more likely you'll implement a strategy to achieve it.

The clearer your desired outcome, the more likely you'll implement a strategy to achieve it.

The only time a trade fails is when it's inequitable—when the capital you give up far outweighs what you gain. Being intentional ensures you make trades that align with your values and lead to long-term fulfillment.

Questions:

1. Which capital do you need to invest in most right now?

2. What would it look like to use your other capitals to grow that area?

The 5 Capitals in Practice

Life is all about trading and investing one or more of the 5 Capitals, whether we realize it or not. Every interaction, every decision involves an exchange. The challenge is making sure those trades reflect your values and your long-term goals. The 5 Capitals tool helps you stay intentional and strategic, ensuring that the investments you're making today are leading you to a future you'll be proud of.

TAKEAWAYS

- We are finite beings managing finite resources. Every "yes" to one thing is a "no" to something else.

- Each day, we make decisions about how to invest our time, energy, and resources with the hope of achieving a meaningful ROI.

- The 5 Capitals are like the five main bank accounts you have in life, and they are expressed in different currencies.

- If you want to grow one of the 5 Capitals, you need to leverage the others.

REFLECTION QUESTIONS

- Take the time to review the questions throughout this chapter. Write your answers down and review them in three months. How are you doing?

UNLOCKING YOUR FULL LEADERSHIP POTENTIAL

L eadership is one of life's most exhilarating, challenging, and rewarding journeys. As you've read through this book, you've encountered a range of tools designed to elevate your leadership performance, optimize your impact, and unlock your full potential. Each tool—whether it was the EQ Matrix, the Development Square, or the Trust Code—has been carefully crafted to help you build the kind of leadership that leaves a lasting legacy. But let's be clear: these tools are only as powerful as they are integrated into our lives.

The MPWR LOS is more than a set of tools; it's a transformative framework that turns potential into tangible results. This system is about putting you in control of your leadership journey, enabling you to create meaningful change in your life, your team, and your organization. It's about empowering you to lead with clarity, consistency, and conviction—whether you're navigating tough decisions, fostering strong relationships, or driving business outcomes.

As you move forward, I want to challenge you to ask yourself one key question: How will you activate these tools in your life?

The Truth About Transformation

Here's the truth—just reading about these tools won't make you a great leader. They won't magically transform your life overnight or solve all your problems with a wave of a wand. Real transformation requires action, accountability, and often, guidance from someone who can see the bigger picture. It requires doing the hard work of self-reflection, practice, and consistent improvement. And most of all, it requires humility—the willingness to admit that even the best leaders have blind spots and need a coach to challenge, guide, and support them on their journey.

Every great leader has someone who helps them see what they can't see, holds them accountable to their vision, and pushes them to keep growing.

I know this from personal experience and from the hundreds of leaders I've had the privilege of coaching. No matter how experienced or talented they are, the leaders who truly succeed are the ones who embrace coaching. They understand that greatness isn't a solo journey. It's a team effort. Every athlete has a coach. Every artist has a mentor. Every great leader has someone who helps them see what they can't see, holds them accountable to their vision, and pushes them to keep growing.

That's where I come in.

The Power of Coaching

Imagine the impact of having a coach who understands where you're going and helps you navigate the path to get there. Imagine having someone by your side who not only challenges you to be better but gives you the precise tools and insights to make it happen. What would that kind of accountability, expertise, and partnership mean for you?

Here's what coaching offers that you can't get from simply reading a book or attending a seminar:

1. Personalized Guidance: I'll help you take the tools from this book and apply them to your unique leadership challenges and goals. It's one thing to understand the concepts, but coaching makes them relevant to your real-life situations.

2. Objective Feedback: The hardest part of leadership is seeing yourself clearly. I provide an outside perspective that helps you uncover blind spots, identify opportunities for growth, and avoid pitfalls you might not even see coming.

3. Accountability: Transformation doesn't happen by accident. It happens when someone holds you accountable for your goals and pushes you to follow through, even when it's uncomfortable.

4. Real Results: Whether you want to scale your business, improve team dynamics, or increase personal fulfillment, coaching accelerates your progress. I've seen leaders go from stuck to thriving, not because they had all the answers, but because they were willing to invest in themselves and commit to growth.

What's Next?

If you've made it this far in the book, you're already ahead of the game. You're someone who is committed to being a better leader, and that's exactly the kind of person who benefits most from coaching. The question now is: Are you ready to take the next step?

Working with me is about more than just learning new skills or strategies—it's about unlocking your full potential as a leader and a human being. It's about maximizing your impact, creating a legacy, and ensuring that you're living and leading in alignment with your core values. It's about becoming the kind of leader people want to follow because they trust you, respect you, and are inspired by you.

Your Leadership Journey Starts Now

The MPWR LOS is just the beginning. The real journey begins when you decide to activate these tools and invest in yourself. Don't let this book be another resource you put on the shelf, only to gather dust. Let it be the start of something powerful.

So, what's your next step? If you're serious about growing as a leader, then I invite you to explore how coaching can take you there faster and more effectively. Let's unlock your potential together, using the MPWR LOS as the roadmap to guide your journey.

Take Action

If you're ready to elevate your leadership and create lasting change, I'm here to help. Schedule a consultation with me **(www.mpwrcoaching.com),** and let's talk about how coaching can help you implement the tools from this book, break through barriers, and achieve the success you deserve.

Remember, the best leaders are those who never stop learning, growing, and investing in themselves. Let's unlock your potential and create the legacy you were meant to leave.

Let's do this together.

RECOMMENDED RESOURCES

These works from which I have leaned upon, gleaned insights from, adapted concepts and support the core principles and practices reflected in this book. I recommend all of these works for a further exploration of what it means to be a leader worth following!

Adair, J. (2009). *Not Bosses but Leaders: How to Lead the Way to Success*. Kogan Page.

Blanchard, K. (1985). *Leadership and the One-Minute Manager: Increasing Effectiveness Through Situational Leadership*. William Morrow.

Bradberry, T., & Greaves, J. (2009). *Emotional Intelligence 2.0*. TalentSmart.

Breen, M. (2011). *Building a Discipling Culture*. 3DM.

Breen, M. (2012). *Multiplying Missional Leaders: From Halfhearted Volunteers to a Mobilized Kingdom Force*. 3DM Publishing.

Breen, M. (2015). *Oikonomics: How to Invest in Life's Five Capitals the Way Jesus Did*. 3DM.

Brown, B. (2018). *Dare to Lead: Brave Work. Tough Conversations. Whole Hearts*. Random House.

Chapman, G. (1992). *The 5 Love Languages: The Secret to Love That Lasts*. Northfield Publishing.

Covey, S. R. (1989). *The 7 Habits of Highly Effective People: Powerful Lessons in Personal Change*. Simon & Schuster.

Csikszentmihalyi, M. (1990). *Flow: The Psychology of Optimal Experience*. Harper & Row.

Dweck, C. S. (2006). *Mindset: The New Psychology of Success*. Random House.

Goldsmith, M. (2007). *What Got You Here Won't Get You There: How Successful People Become Even More Successful*. Hyperion.

Heath, C., & Heath, D. (2010). *Switch: How to Change Things When Change is Hard*. Broadway Books.

Keller, G., & Papasan, J. (2013). *The One Thing: The Surprisingly Simple Truth Behind Extraordinary Results*. Bard Press.

Lencioni, P. (2002). *The Five Dysfunctions of a Team: A Leadership Fable*. Jossey-Bass.

McKeown, G. (2014). *Essentialism: The Disciplined Pursuit of Less*. Crown Business.

Rock, D. (2009). *Your Brain at Work: Strategies for Overcoming Distraction, Regaining Focus, and Working Smarter All Day Long*. HarperBusiness.

Scazzero, P. (2017). *Emotionally Healthy Leadership: How Transforming Your Inner Life will Deeply Transform Your Church, Team, and the World*. Zondervan.

Schwartz, T. (2010). *The Way We're Working isn't Working: The Four Forgotten Needs that Energize Great Performance.* Free Press.

Shirky, C. (2010). *Cognitive Surplus: Creativity and Generosity in a Connected Age.* Penguin Press.

Sinek, S. (2009). *Start with Why: How Great Leaders Inspire Everyone to Take Action.* Portfolio.

Smith, R. H. (1998). *The Wizard of Ads: Turning Words into Magic and Dreamers into Millionaires.* Bard Press.

www.ingramcontent.com/pod-product-compliance
Lightning Source LLC
Chambersburg PA
CBHW071559210326
41597CB00019B/3313